Keepers of Salt

By Debby Davis

Lasting Covenants in a World of Broken Promises

Forward by Paul Johansson

Keepers of Salt by Deborah Lee Davis
Published by Davis Mission
116 North 12th Street
Olean New York 14760
E-mail Address: debby@davismission.com

Copyright © 2004 by Deborah Lee Davis
All Rights Reserved
Second Edition 2007
Printed in the United States of America

All Scripture is quoted from the Authorized Version of the King James Bible unless otherwise noted.

Cover Design By ART & INK
Cathy Hoffman and Shirley Condon
Emporium , Pennsylvania

DEDICATION

It is with great joy that I dedicate this, my second book, to my Blood Covenant Friend, Jesus. "Greater love has no man then he lay down his life for his friends." Jesus laid down His life for me and He calls me His friend. He is the reason I live and the joy of my life.

Secondly, I dedicate this book to my husband, Fred. This year, he and I celebrated twenty-five years of our Covenant Friendship. He has been my sweetheart, my companion and my Covenant friend. I have been blessed with many friends, but he is the one I chose twenty-five years ago and he is still the best.

TABLE OF CONTENTS

FORWARD

As Christians who live with the anticipation of the Second Coming of the Lord Jesus Christ, we become more aware of the signs of the times. Seeing the broken society around us while we hear of "wars and rumors of wars", we are made aware these are truly the last days. Paul's words in 1 Thessalonians 5:3, "When they say, 'Peace, peace' then sudden destruction will come upon them," is fulfilled today in the land where they were uttered. However a more subtle warning of the last days that has been given, from 11 Timothy 3:3 is, "they shall be trucebreakers." In other words, those who do not keep their covenants. It is to this evil that Debby draws attention in Keepers of Salt.

I have had the privilege of knowing Debby since her early Bible School days. She has always impressed me as a young lady with a heart for God. From the concerns she requested prayer for, it was obvious she had a heart to see healing where there had been damaged relationships and wounded spirits. It is to this healing that covenant (salt) must be applied.

Keepers of Salt has been written in a way that flows with warm illustrations of the need for healing where covenants have been broken. Using the divine pattern, Debby finds a way to bring the natural covenants of marriage, church membership, and friendship to a higher level. Her illustrations come from many different sources, including their rich experiences in West Africa.

After reading this book myself, I was deeply moved by a God who keeps this covenant. May this volume bring the reader to a sharpening of his convictions and a strengthening of his relationships, so that he remains a divine object lesson to the world in covenant keeping. May he not be so influenced by the world that he accepts their lifestyle, which, in many cases, would erode his ability to be "Keepers of Salt".

I recommend this book for it brings us back to a covenant keeping God who sent his Son to redeem us to be His covenant keeping people.

Reverend Paul Johansson
President Elim Bible Institute
Lima New York

Special Thanks

This book would not have been possible without the great help of three people. Dani Burket was one of the first to sit and listen to me as I wrote and rewrote all of my stories. So that I would have more time to write, she also home schooled our daughter, Marie-Louise, and spent time reading and proofing my rough draft. My husband Fred listened to me as I read and reread my stories to him. He gave me ideas and listened to change after change. Then he spent many hours formatting and getting everything ready for print. My son Christopher showed me the greatest love and patience as he spent well over a hundred hours editing. He sacrificed much of his summer and Christmas vacation time working with me on this manuscript. He is a great editor and this book is a reflection of his hard work and patience.

I want to thank Dr Ken and Judy Mundy, Lou and Thelma Goszleth, Becky Ingole, Gigi St.John, Peggy Schultz, Ruth Crevlin, Gloria Smith and Cathy Hoffman for listening to me, proofing, helping me with pull quotes and encouraging me in this project. Cathy also worked many hours, taking hundreds of pictures for the cover; her creativity and vision has been very encouraging. My mom and dad and sister Cheri have also been invaluable in teaching me Covenant and encouraging me in this project. I also want to thank all those whose lives have enriched my life; their stories are an integral part of this book. Thank you!

Most of all I want to thank my eternal Covenant Friend Jesus, for giving His life that I might live. His Covenant sacrifice has changed my life and I am so thankful for Him.

PREFACE

The night was dark and stormy. The wind was blowing, and tensions were high. The storm didn't rage just on the outside of the boat, but inside too, as all of the animals began to criticize and complain about each other to Noah. The time was two weeks after God had shut the door of the ark.

Misses Cat came to Noah; with her prissy little voice she said, "Mr. Noah, did you know there was a dog on this boat?"

Noah replied, "Why, yes I did. I even helped him on board. What's wrong with the dog?"

"Well you see Mr. Noah, I have my baby kitties to think about and that dog just keeps looking at them. I know he's up to no good. He has a bad reputation. I have heard stories about him. I know you think you have done well to invite him on your boat, but after all, we do have the children to think about! You can't mix cats and dogs. I think he should leave and if he doesn't, I will!"

Noah took Misses cat by the paw and led her up to the window at the top of the ark. After opening the window, he lifted the cat so she could see. Then he said, "You have a problem because the dog is going to stay. If you want to leave, out there is the only place you can go!"

Looking outside at the dark and stormy rage, the cat shuddered as her hair stood up on end. She turned to Noah and said, "I guess that old dog isn't as bad as I thought. I think I'll stay."

Noah thought his problems were over until he turned and saw that many of the other animals had problems as well.

Madam Duck arrived, much concerned because the monkeys had been playing with her baby ducks. "Mr. Noah, I raised my children well. Have you noticed how they march all in a row? Well, just two weeks playing with those monkeys and they're all over the boat. It's going to take me weeks to retrain them. I think the monkeys should go. If they don't, I will!"

Nobody liked the skunk. The porcupine was needling everyone. The lion had a big mouth. The parrots were the biggest gossips. The elephant was always rocking the boat. And of course, no one could stand the peacock; he was so proud everyone was sick of him!

One by one, Noah took them up to the window. Showing them the darkness and death, Noah would ask them, "Do you want to stay here with all of us, or go out there? This is the only boat that floats. It's your choice."

Trembling with fear, each one of the animals backed away in shame from the window and decided to stay.

Growing up, I often heard my father relate this story when he was trying to "drive home" a specific point. What I have come to discover is that the church is much like my dad's tale of the animals in Noah's ark. Yes there are problems, but the church is the only boat that floats. The Family of God is our place of safety. It is the ark provided in the midst of life's dark and stormy rage. Jesus Himself is the door. He is our Eternal Covenant and all of those who are inside His house are in Covenant with Him and with each other.

We are like Peter who said to Jesus, "Where else can we go? You alone have the Words of Eternal Life!." (**John 6 :68**) We need the church. There is no other place for us to go. You may not like everyone in the church but it's the only place to be. It's the only "boat that floats"!

Years ago, a new couple visited our church. They had been married for more than twenty years and had three children. Their oldest daughter was married, so this added a son-in-law and two grandchildren. My husband Fred and I thought they would be a great addition to our church. Having just moved to our area, Matt and Jane[1] were anxious to be involved and become an active part of our church fellowship.

Everyone in the church was excited to see a new family. It didn't take long before we were all friends. They seemed like the ideal family. Matt had a great job and worked hard. Jane loved to read the Bible and was always sharing something the Lord had shown her in her time of devotions.

One night at prayer meeting Jane shared some family problems. Her daughter had some troubles in her marriage. It seemed like problems had plagued the daughter's marriage from the start. Then Jane told us that her own marriage was strained. She and her husband had been arguing for years and were slowly drifting apart.

For weeks and months we prayed for both couples but their situations didn't seem to change. We would gather together and pray with all of our hearts. We knew that God heard our prayers, yet no matter how much we prayed, Jane's family situation remained unresolved. Jane shared how she spent hours praying and believing God for solutions. Soon the prayer requests included their teenage son, who was now experimenting with alcohol and drugs, and the grandchildren who were having emotional problems and trouble at school.

I learned that Matt and Jane had been members in several churches in the ten years since they had given their lives to Jesus. Unfortunately, disagreements and offences had shortened their average length of stay in any given church to about two years. This really surprised me since this couple had so much to offer. Why did their life seem to continually revolve around problems and offences? Why couldn't they ever become established in one church? Why couldn't they maintain any victory in their lives?

I knew that God was able to help Matt and Jane. I also knew that Jane was a real prayer warrior. I often heard her tell how she would spend hours at a time praying. For some reason however their situation only got worse. Soon their daughter and her husband divorced, their son continued in his wild lifestyle, and eventually Matt and Jane became offended and left our church. Why wasn't their situation changing? Was something missing? Doesn't Christianity work? Does God still answer prayer? Like Matt and Jane, many people are longing for a place to fit in. They go from church to church hoping to find acceptance and love. Yet because of offences and wounded hearts, people often close the doors of their hearts, and build high walls intended to keep others out. Then they wander from place to place, looking for the

Family of God, wondering if it even exists. Why does this happen? What are we doing wrong? Why are our prayers left unanswered?

In his book, *The Salt Covenant*, Dr. H. Clay Trumbull describes the significance of Salt Covenants. In Bible days, a Salt Covenant was like a contract that could never be broken. It was perpetual and unchangeable[2]. Dr. Trumbull also describes two different types of people, *spillers of salt* as people who break friendships, and *abusers of salt* as people who cannot be trusted to keep their agreements[3]. Wouldn't it be wonderful if we could be people who never break our friendships and who can always be trusted to keep our word? Wouldn't it be a powerful testimony to the world if our Covenants were like those of the Salt Covenants, perpetual and unchangeable? Instead of being *spillers* or *abusers* of salt, we would be **Keepers of Salt**, a people of Covenant.

This book is a story of Covenant. *Covenant* is the missing key to abundant blessings and answered prayer. The hidden secret to a fruitful and victorious Christian life, *Covenant* brings resolution to the kinds of troubles Matt and Jane faced. *Covenant* will change your life and also revolutionize your thinking, challenging you to a deeper commitment with Christ and with His Body, the Church.

This book chronicles my journey towards a deep friendship with God that can only be found in perpetual and unchangeable Covenant. My first step was when I asked the Lord to share one of the secrets of His heart. My pilgrimage began when he answered with one word, "Covenant". I believe that Covenant is a key that will release the power and build the unity we need in the church.

I believe that if we begin to walk in Covenant relationships, Jesus' prayer "that all of them would be one" will be fulfilled in our generation. (**John 17:21**) We will see God move in signs and wonders. We will see the People of God rise up and be strong. We will see the Body of Christ emerge as a glorious bride, carried over the threshold of Covenant by her groom.

We will be "Keepers of Salt"!

John 17:20-23

Neither pray I for these alone, but for them also which shall believe on me through their word; that they all may be one; as thou, Father, art in me, and I in thee, that they also may be one in us: that the world may believe that thou hast sent me. And the glory which thou gavest me I have given them; that they may be one, even as we are one: I in them, and thou in me, that they may be made perfect in one; and that the world may know that thou hast sent me, and hast loved them, as thou hast loved me.

All heaven stands ready to enforce every Covenant Right of yours when you dare to be bold in claiming them.

— T.L. Osborn

A true friend is forever a friend.

— George Macdonald

CHAPTER 1

COVENANTS FOREVER

Two men sat across from each other. The younger man was intensely observing the older. Past animosity plagued the unspoken distance between them. Their families had been enemies for generations. The tension of their current encounter had already lasted for what seemed like hours, each man wondering what would happen next. Finally their eyes met as the older man raised his head. Then the younger man began to speak. His arms were strong and tanned from his hard work in the fields. His eyes were needy and pleading.

"Listen, I know that there have been bad feelings between my tribe and yours, but times are changing. I need your influence and position. I have worked hard and I have proven myself. It is time we ended our differences. I want a Covenant with you. I need you. I'll give my life for you."

The older man bowed his gray head, and thought for a moment before he spoke. Then he lifted his watery eyes and said, "I need you too. I have been watching you for these last few years. Yes, it is time to settle our differences. In three days we shall meet. I'll bring my witnesses, and you bring yours. We shall make a Covenant and bind our lives and families together."

Three days later, a room full of witnesses listened as the two men began to promise honesty, faithfulness, and love to each other. They promised to honor the other's life, and become like one man. The younger man promised to guard the life of the older and care for his needs as he grew even older. The older man promised to share his influence and wisdom, which was greatly desired by the younger. They offered forgiveness for the things of the past. Their Covenant changed a future that had been darkened by hate, into a destiny now bright and full of hope.

After declaring their promises, each began to proclaim awful curses should he ever break this new Covenant. Everyone listened as the younger man declared, "If I ever break this Covenant, I will become poor, and lose all respect from other men. My enemies will overtake me, I will die of a terrible disease and my children will suffer and die as well. This will be the result of my broken Covenant.

When the older man had finished proclaiming his curses, should he ever break the Covenant, they each took out a small pouch that had been tied to their belts. In each pouch was a measure of salt. The older man was the first to remove a pinch of salt. Eager for the Covenant to be completed quickly, the younger man removed a pinch of salt from his pouch as well. They exchanged the salt, putting it in the other man's pouch.

Having done this, they each understood that they had become one in a Salt Covenant. As impossible as it was to separate their grains from the other's pouch, so also would it be impossible for them, as newly made Covenant brothers, to be separated. They were bound in an eternal and unbreakable Covenant.

SALT COVENANTS

Although the thought of exchanging grains of salt may seem strange, further exploration into the underlying spiritual ties with Biblical culture can help us understand this custom. In early Bible times, a man's word was highly valued, to be kept at all costs. To signify the importance of their promise, people often practiced a custom of exchanging salt, which would symbolically seal their promise. The custom was called a "Covenant of Salt". In anticipation of Covenant making, Men wore a pouch of salt tied to their belt. When the time came to make a Covenant, each man would exchange a pinch of salt, putting his grains of salt into the other's pouch. If one of the men attempted to break his Covenant, then the other would respond by saying, "You can break the Covenant if you can retrieve your grains of salt, and yours only, from my

> *"You can break the Covenant if you can retrieve your grains of salt, and yours only, from my pouch". A Salt Covenant was a promise that could never be broken. It was perpetual and unchangeable.*

pouch". Obviously this was impossible because one could not tell his salt from another's. The grains of salt would all become "as one" when they were mixed together. A Covenant that was clearly understood between men in ancient times, symbolized loyalty, honesty, and friendship. It represented that which was a lasting, preserved Covenant.[1] A Salt Covenant was a promise that could never be broken, perpetual and unchangeable.

Salt played a central role at solemn meals where men made Covenants.[2] In ancient times, men would pay special attention to when and where they ate salt. For example, they would never eat salt in the home of someone they didn't want to be in Covenant with. Even tasting salt on their tongue would seal an unbreakable Covenant with the man of the house.[3] Many scholars believe Dr. H. Clay Trumbull to be the greatest authority on Covenant making. Dr Trumbull states in one of his books that "It was dangerous to give away salt to a stranger, because salt is as blood and as life. One must be careful lest he put his blood and his life in the power of an enemy."[4] Regardless of intention, animosity or future offenses, a Salt Covenant could not be broken!

Salt also played a significant role in marriages. Even to this day some people practice Salt Covenants in marriage ceremonies. A perfect example of this, is my friend Salomon. One day he came to our house with exciting news. He was going to get married! We were so happy for him. He had been one of our first students to graduate from our Bible school in Cote d'Ivoire, West Africa, when I began to ask him about the details of his upcoming marriage, he told me that his fiancé was from the tribe of Dida. Traditionally, when a young man asks for the hand of a young Didan woman in marriage, he is obligated to bring a bag of salt with him. Other dowry gifts are happily received, but are not required and may be forgotten. The salt however is compulsorily. The salt is then distributed among all the women of the family. No matter what, the groom can not forget the salt.[5] The salt is important because it is the symbol of Covenant.

Jesus too recognized the value of salt in Covenant making. According to Dr. Trumbull, Jesus was talking about Covenants when He said in **Matthew 5:13** that we are "the salt of the earth". Jesus was literally saying that we are God's expression of Covenant to the world. If we break our Covenants or lose our "saltiness", we are worthless. The recognized meaning of a Salt Covenant in Jesus' day consequently intensified the importance of Jesus' words.[6] Has the Church, today, lost it's saltiness? The world watches the Church and gains an understanding of who God really is when God's people uphold their Covenants. When God's people break their Covenants, the world no longer sees a Covenant keeping God. Instead they see a religious social club, a powerless church without God.

GOD, THE COVENANT MAKER

God is a Covenant making God. **Titus 1:2** tells us that before the beginning of time, God made the Covenant of eternal life.[7] To God, Covenant was a prerequisite for all creation, even time. Before "in the beginning", there was Covenant. God values Covenant above all.

Jeremiah 33:20-22; 25-26, gives an account of the Covenant that God made concerning day and night.[8] From the very beginning of time there has been day and night, and God has never broken this Covenant. Every day starts and ends the same. God has maintained this Covenant even to this day. Jeremiah shows us how these first two Covenants, eternal life and day and night, are tied together.

Thus saith the LORD; If ye can break my Covenant of the day, and my Covenant of the night, and that there should not be day and night in their season; Then may also my Covenant be broken with David my servant, that he should not have a son to reign upon his throne; and with the Levites the priests, my ministers. As the host of heaven cannot be numbered, neither the sand of the sea measured: so will I multiply the seed of David my servant, and the Levites that minister unto me. Thus saith the LORD; If my Covenant be not with day and night, and if I have not appointed the ordinances of heaven and earth; Then will I cast away the seed of Jacob, and David my servant, so that I will not take any of his seed to be rulers over the seed of Abraham, Isaac, and Jacob: for I will cause their captivity to return, and have mercy on them. **Jeremiah 30:20-22, 25-26**

Not only did God make a Covenant with day and night, but also with the seasons, the sun, the moon and the stars. He established this Covenant again with Noah.[9] He promised that as long as the earth remained, there would be spring and fall, summer and winter, day and night. This became an unbreakable, unchangeable Covenant. If this Covenant was able to be broken, then the Covenant with David could also be broken. In **II Chronicles 13:5**, the Covenant with David was called a **Covenant of Salt**. There would forever be a Son of David upon the throne. This Covenant is fulfilled in Jesus, Who is the King of

Israel for all eternity. Since the Covenant of day and night will never be broken, we have confidence that our Covenant of eternal life will never be broken. Day and night is our token of God's faithfulness. Every day when you wake up and see the sun, remember that this is part of God's eternal Covenant.

COVENANT FRIENDSHIP

God wanted His Covenant nature to become a part of man. We read in **Genesis** that God created man and desired to walk in Covenant with him. God's desire was for a deep friendship with Adam. However, Adam rejected God's Covenant. Adam, as Dr. Trumbull describes, became like a *spiller of salt*. Imagine the symbolism of Adam taking the forbidden fruit with one hand, and spilling precious grains of salt with the other. From that day until this day, God has desired a restoration of Covenant Friendship with man.

Let's examine the significant connection between salt, blood and friendship. In Bible days, salt and blood were used interchangeably in Covenant ceremonies.[10] Both blood and salt can represent Covenant and they also represent life because blood has salt in it. In fact, blood and salt were recognized so closely in Latin that the two words come from the same root.[11] Throughout the Bible we see clearly the recorded Covenants God made with man. The Covenant with Abraham and his descendants is the most remarkable, sealed with both the blood of a substitutionary animal in the place of God's blood, and the blood of Abraham through circumcision.[12] This was how God and Abraham entered into Blood Covenant Friendship.

Dr. H. Clay Trumbull and another well-respected author, E. W. Kenyon, affirm in their writings the ancient Biblical acts of Covenanting which we have described so far.[13] Trumbull showed that even before the days of Abraham and for centuries thereafter, man has offered Blood and Salt Covenants. This was a normal, understood way of life. In his study on Blood Covenant, Jack Hayford, he states that Covenant is one of the key elements of the Bible.[14] The very nature of God is represented in His Covenant acts. In fact, Kevin Conner and Ken Malmin, in their book, *The Covenants*, argue that Covenant is critical to understanding the foundation of the Bible itself.

Abraham was called the friend of God.[15] He is the first and only person in the Old Testament who received this honor. Moses talked face to face with God, but was never called God's friend. David had a heart after God's heart, but was never called God's friend. Elisha, Samuel and Isaiah walked with God and knew His voice, but none were called the friend of God. Only Abraham was called *a friend.* I have often tried to pattern my life after the great men and women of the Bible. Each one has unique characteristics and is a wonderful example. Their remarkable relationships with God are what I desire. Above all, I desire the unique friendship with God that only Abraham found. He experienced Blood Covenant Friendship.

Abraham became God's friend through the power of Covenant.[16] God blessed Abraham and vowed to make him the father of many nations. Kings would come from him, the whole land of Canaan would be his, and his seed would be blessed. His descendants would become like sand on the seashore and stars in the sky.[17] We see in **Galatians 3:14** that the Covenant blessings of Abraham are also for us! God's plan from the beginning of time has been to share this Covenant with us. But more than just blessings, God's desire for us is Covenant friendship. He created the world for the sole purpose of developing Covenant friendship with us. God's Covenant with us is unchangeable. He can be trusted. He is Faithful. God is a **Keeper of Salt.**

Covenants like the one between Abraham and God are few indeed, remaining scarce even in the church today. Jesus prayed that His body (the church) would all be one. The process of becoming "one" is brought about by faithful men and women, making lasting Covenants which cannot be broken by offenses, hurts or disappointments.

> *Covenants like the one between Abraham and God are few indeed, and these type of Covenants remain scarce even in the church today.*

BLOOD COVENANTS

The Hebrew word for Covenant means *to cut,* coming from a time when two men would cut their flesh and mingle their blood to symbolize that they had become one. Used over two hundred and fifty times in the Old Testament alone, the word it's self means "to cut" a Covenant, or make a Blood Covenant [18]. Blood Covenants, like Salt Covenants, could never be broken or changed.[19] They were forever.

In my travels I have found that even today there are people in Africa who practice blood Covenanting. In the country of Benin in West Africa, for example, one of the mayors in the largest city, Cotonou, has bound his cabinet ministers with a blood Covenant oath. His cabinet swore allegiance to their mayor by cutting themselves, pouring their blood in a common cup and then drinking the mingled blood.[20] In Abidjan, Cote d'Ivoire, I attended a church service where a former witch shared her testimony about her Covenant with Satan. According to her, she washed her face every day with blood. She did this to reaffirm her Blood Covenant with demonic powers. I have been told that this is a common practice among those in witchcraft.

THE OBLIGATIONS OF COVENANT

In ancient times, the ceremonies of Blood and Salt Covenanting included all of the essential ingredients needed to establish a Covenant: words, the sacrifice and the seal. Words included the promises of blessing and cursing, terms of the Covenant, and the oath. The sacrifice of the Covenant would be blood, salt or wine. The seal of the Covenant could be anything that was a tangible witness to the Covenant, such as the bag of exchanged salt, a ring, amulet or the Holy Spirit. [21]

Obligations are a critical key to understanding Covenant. Failure to meet obligations results in a curse. For example, Abraham was presented with two obligations in his Covenant with God. First, God told Abraham to walk before Him and to be blameless.[22] The Bible does not say specifically, but we can infer that failure to meet this obligation would have resulted in loss of blessings or even a curse. Second, God required Abraham's act of circumcision.[23] Through this act, Abraham willingly cut his own body in a Blood Covenant to establish his friendship with God. Just like Abraham, Jesus also willingly gave His body in a blood Covenant for us. However, to become Jesus' friends and receive all the blessings of Abraham, we are obligated to circumcise our hearts.

In **Deuteronomy**, we read of a new generation of Israel who were ready to follow Joshua into the land of Covenant. God used the *language of Covenant*, which we will discuss later, to speak promises to His people. They would be blessed wherever they went. They would be the head and not the tail. Their children would be blessed, and their enemies would flee from them. However, to receive the blessings of this Covenant, Israel was obligated to be faithful and to serve God with all of their hearts. The consequences of failing to meet these obligations included curses and loss of blessing. They would suffer from horrible diseases, and their enemies would make them their slaves. Nothing would ever go right for them. In **Chapter 28**, there are more than twenty-five blessings, but there are more than sixty curses for those who break the Covenant. Interestingly, Deuteronomy is the only book Jesus quoted when he was tempted in the desert. [24] Obviously Jesus recognized the value of the Covenant and the power it contained. Just as Covenant gave Jesus authority to overcome Satan, it is Covenant that gives us the same authority today.

FROM COVENANT TO CURSE

The book of **Judges** has a consistent Covenant theme. Not only did the children of Israel forget the great truths that the Lord had done, they forgot to tell those great things to their children. [25] They forgot the Covenant. Forgotten Covenants lead to broken Covenants and broken Covenants lead to curses. The reality of a curse is that it is the opposite, or absence of blessings. As a result of Israel's forgetfulness, they walked in the curses of broken Covenant and were repeatedly sold into slavery and bondage. Israel's suffering was never the desire of God; it was a situation they had brought upon themselves. Israel's disregard for Covenants certainly made God sad, yet we see in scripture that God always had mercy on them when they were suffering.

Curses are the natural consequences following those who do not keep the Covenant. As New Testament Christians, we don't like to use the word curse. We think curses

> *Forgotten Covenants lead to broken Covenants. broken Covenants lead to curses. The reality of a curse is that it is the opposite, or absence of blessings.*

don't apply to us, but this is a real part of Covenant. For Covenant breakers, not only will the blessings of Covenant not be available, but a curse will follow. In the Bible, if a person was unfaithful to a Covenant, they were guilty of an enormous crime. The Apostle Paul describes Covenant breakers in **Romans 1:31**, as people whose minds are depraved and are filled with every kind of wickedness.[26]

Have you ever broken a dish? Covenant breakers are like dish breakers. You may own a beautiful set of imported china, but if you break one cup, you lose the benefit of that piece. If you break all of the pieces, all of the benefits of the china are lost. Yes, the set of dishes are still yours, and you can look at them thinking about how pretty they were and how expensive they were to buy. You can talk about them to your friends, but you can't use them. They are broken! As a child of God you hold in your heart all of the wonderful, costly blessings and promises paid for by the blood of Jesus. God's Covenant nature confines Him to the laws of Covenant. So, if you break your Covenant, you have just tied God's hands. God will not override the law of Covenant to give you your blessing. Just like you may own a broken dish, a broken promise is a lost blessing, rendered useless because of *your* broken Covenant. Just think what happens when you break all of your Covenants? No wonder some of us have little joy and satisfaction in our lives, as well as ineffective prayers.

COVENANTS, THE MINGLING OF OUR HEARTS

What does Covenant mean for us today? Does God expect us to make Covenants? Are there blessings and curses today? Does God look for us to make a Covenant of friendship with Him like Abraham did? Does He want us to make Covenants with others in His Body, and would *this* finally fulfill His prayer that we would become one? Do you believe that God wants *you* to make a Covenant with Him? Does God expect you to make a Covenant with His Body as well? Are you living under curses of broken Covenants? Do your blessings seem to be slipping through your fingers?

Years ago, I overheard someone ask an elderly Baptist lady why she stayed in her church. Problems within the church body had caused others to leave. Her response was, "I was born a Baptist and I will die a Baptist." She didn't care if she liked the way things were. She didn't care if she liked or disliked the pastor. She was a Baptist, and she intended to stay that way! I wonder if this kind of commitment is missing in our churches today. Yes, I know there are truly terrible things that happen in some churches. Instead of trusting and believing God to change the situations, we have made leaving too easy. Like the two men at the beginning of the chapter who shared salt, we have shared our salt with others in the Body of Christ. When we separate or break our relationships and Covenants, it is impossible to gather all of our grains from the other's pouch. Because our Covenants have mingled our hearts, the separations have left many in the Body of Christ wounded and bleeding. Perhaps this is why we have become weak and powerless, while the world laughs at us much as they laughed at the children of Israel in the Book of Judges.

I have often wondered what Jesus meant when He said, "Greater works than these shall ye do because I go unto my Father". [27] Frustrated, I looked at my life and the lives of those around me, and realized that we were not doing the greater works. I have wondered and questioned why. Why don't I see the greater works? Why are they not evident in my life? I know what Jesus said is true, and that God is able. The problem is not with God, so the problem has to be with me. What am I missing? What is wrong that I don't see these "greater works"? In my search I have begun to look at Covenant. I thought I understood Covenant. I grew up in church, went to Bible school, and had read the Bible many times, but I really didn't understand Covenant.

David says, in **Psalm 25:14**, "The secret of the LORD is with them who fear Him, and He will show them His **Covenant.**" Do you want to know God's secret? I believe that the secret of the Lord can be found when we become Covenant Keepers. Keepers enjoy all the blessings of Covenant while breakers walk on the glass of their own broken promises. As we begin to recognize the power and blessings of Covenant, we will see the blessings we so desire and thus curses will fall away.

We will become **Keepers of Salt**!

> *Keepers enjoy all the blessings of Covenant while breakers walk on the glass of their own broken promises.*

We cannot expect the world to believe that the Father sent the Son, that Jesus' claims are true, and that Christianity is true, unless the world sees some reality of oneness of true Christians.

— Francis Schaeffer

CHAPTER 2

STRONG FRIENDSHIP

John MacGregor, more commonly known as Rob Roy, was the Scottish Robin Hood, or Robin the Red. A Scottish hero who fought for the independence of Scotland from the English. He was imprisoned by the English in the 1720s. He also invented the competitive sport of Canoeing. Stories of his life are legendary.

While canoeing on the Jordan River, John was taken captive by a band of hostile Arabs. Sitting in one of their dusty tents, John eyed his captors. In a desperate attempt to save his life, John pulled out a small box from his belongings. Opening it up, he displayed a fine white powder. He held some in his hand, offering it to the leader of the group. Thinking the powder was sugar, the Arab leader took some and tasted it. Immediately John also took some of the white powder and quickly put it in his mouth as well. He laughed in a loud voice, clapping the Arab on the back. The powder was refined salt! The two had just eaten Salt together, which meant they had just entered into a Salt Covenant.

The Arab looked shocked. Those around him began to ask, "What happened? Was it sugar?" The Arab sheepishly replied, "It was salt!"

Everyone in the room laughed for John had out-smarted the Arab, in his own tent. Now a Salt Covenant, the strongest tie, bound them.

The Arabs escorted John and his canoe back to the Jordan River. He was free to go, for they could no longer keep him. Not only that, they sent him away with shouts of peace and blessing. He was their Covenant brother now and nothing could ever change that fact! [1]

Blood, salt, and even the juice of the grape (the blood of the grape) could be substituted for each other in Covenant ceremonies [2]. For example, in the custom of primitive peoples, blood and salt were recognized as equal. They recognized that both blood and salt were necessary for life; thus they were interchangeable. Even today in hospitals around the world, salt replaces blood in the form of intravenous saline solutions. Primitive people who didn't have salt, or couldn't afford it, would drink blood in order to live [3]. According to Jewish law, Jews were forbidden to drink blood. As a substitution, they used the blood of the grape in Covenant ceremonies. In all these examples, we see that there are three equally binding elements which can be used in Covenant making: salt, blood and the blood of the grape. Each element was equally respected and equally binding.

In the story, the Arab bound himself to MacGregor

when they tasted salt together. This was the equivalent of a Blood Covenant Friendship. Because both parties honored this tradition, MacGregor and the Arab became Covenant brothers, bound in Covenant Friendship. They were then obligated to love each other as themselves. MacGregor's status as an enemy was changed by a Covenant. Animosity was lost while a compulsorily friendship was gained.

Jesus taught us that Communion is a *Covenant oath of friendship*. Just like the story of MacGregor's salt Covenant with the Arab, we also make Covenants each time we participate in Holy Communion. MacGregor and the Arab used salt, we use the blood of the grape. **John 15:15** tell us that after The Last Supper (Communion), Jesus declared "I no longer call you servants, but I call you my friends".

Although we may not realize it, something happens during Communion that changes our status. Like

> *Jesus taught us that Communion is a Covenant oath of friendship.*

MacGregor, whose status was changed from enemy to friend, so we enter into Blood Covenant Friendship with all those with whom we partake Holy Communion.

THE LANGUAGE OF COVENANT

Communion has always been a mystery to many people in the Church. Imagery of Communion often seems so strange that some simply pass it off as antiquated tradition, a symbol that isn't really relevant to us today. In **John 6:53** Jesus said we must "eat His flesh" and "drink His blood". In **Luke 22:19-20** Jesus told us that after He "took bread", He said, "This is My body which is given for you." He then did the same with the cup, saying, "This cup is the New Testament in My blood, which is shed for you". Why did Jesus say something that seemed so offensive and strange? How do we even begin to understand what He was saying since we would never even think of drinking a man's blood or eating His flesh? Jesus' words and message will remain a mystery to us until we begin to understand the language He was using, *the language of Covenant.*

Every family uses their own language. They have secret words, pet names, even the deadly stare from a mother that only her children recognize. Covenant language has its own set of words too. It is a language that directly refers to Covenant acts. When Jesus used Covenant language, His disciples understood. They knew that "eating flesh" and "drinking blood" were acts of Covenant. Jesus was telling them that He wanted to make a Covenant with them. Dr. Trumbull states that, "[Communion] was not an utterly new symbolism that Jesus was introducing…it was rather a new meaning."[4] Trumbull writes that Jesus was talking about a Blood Covenant of Friendship with God.[5] The Disciples understood that Jesus was speaking of Covenant, but they did not realize that Jesus was offering to them the same Blood Covenant Friendship with God that Abraham had.[6]

Jesus' Covenant language was clear to the Disciples. When He took the wine cup, the disciples understood it to be a Covenanting cup. It represented Jesus' life, freely given in Blood Covenant sacrifice. Dr. Trumbull tells us that, Jesus' terminology literally meant that He would become "one" with His Disciples. "When Jesus spoke of bread as His flesh and of the fruit of the vine as His blood, He used terms, that in His day, [formed] the basis of the Covenant by which two become one in a merged common life."[7] Jesus offered Covenant to His disciples in a commonly understood ceremony. The disciples knew that this was a life and death commitment. He was offering them a Blood Covenant of Friendship!

Eating and drinking among the Jews was the privilege of friendship. Jews refused to eat with those who were not their friends because eating was also a form of Covenant making. Jesus wanted His disciples to be His friends. However, Jesus was longing for more than mere relationship, He wanted Covenant friendship. Only a Blood Covenant would express His true love for them.[8] While relationships can be temporary, Covenants bind forever. Jesus was offering them an eternal gift.[9] The happiness of heaven and all spiritual blessings are represented in this image.[10]

COVENANT GOES BEYOND RELATIONSHIP

One of the popular buzzwords today is "relationship". Magazines offer relationship "improvements" while online dating services promise "lasting love". Relationship has become a magic drug, for which everyone is eager to sell his or her prescription. Yet, these prescriptions are ultimately ineffective because they are missing something much more important than mere relationship, Covenant.

I have "relationship" with many people, but I have "Covenant" only with a few. For example, I have a relationship with the headwaiter at our favorite restaurant in Africa. I ask him how he is each time I see him, and he asks me about my friends and family. We talk, and we even have fun when I bring a big crowd to his restaurant. But I don't have a Covenant with him.

We can be in "relationship" without being in "Covenant". We all have simple relationships, but God is looking for us to go one step further. Jesus prayed that we would all be one, not just people sharing a pew on Sunday morning. Jesus prayed that we would make *enduring Covenant Friendships*. This is exactly what Jesus wanted when He offered His disciples the bread and the wine. He wanted Blood Covenant Friends in His greatest time of need, just hours before His crucifixion. He offered a Covenant of oneness, one step further than His disciples had already experienced. He was willing to give His life for them. He was asking them to be willing to do the same.

> *Jesus prayed that we would all be one, not just people sharing a pew on Sunday morning. Jesus prayed that we would make enduring Covenant Friendships.*

Jesus invited the twelve to take the wine and the bread. He didn't ask them to search their hearts. He simply asked them to eat and drink with Him, sealing their binding Covenant of friendship. Jesus even offered Covenant Friendship to Judas, knowing that he would betray Him. It was as if Jesus were pleading with Judas. No, Judas wasn't worthy of Jesus, and Jesus knew that, but He was willing for Judas to come into proper Covenant with Him. Judas was given the opportunity to leave behind his love of money and self-importance. He was invited into an eternal Covenant that, if he would keep it, would change his life forever. And so Jesus offered them all, even Judas, His body and blood. He wanted them to be one with Him. He desired a union that would make them become like He was with His Father, ONE!

COVENANT, GREATER THAN SIN

Some time ago, I was in a dusty little church in West Africa. I listened as the local pastor began to prepare his people for Holy Communion. He asked everyone to open their Bibles to **Mark 14:17-25**. Then the pastor began to read the passage emphasizing the blood and body of Jesus. After reading the passage, he began to exhort the people saying, "Search your heart, and see if you are worthy to take communion. Look and see if there is some hidden sin. If there is, you must deal with it right now. It is dangerous to take Holy Communion with secret sin." He didn't ask if there was anyone who wanted to accept Jesus as his or her Lord and Savior. He didn't ask if there was anyone not in relationship with Jesus. He just told them to look for secret sin.

Was Jesus concerned with secret sin in the Communion story of **Mark 14**? Let's examine this passage together.

And in the evening he cometh with the twelve. And as they sat and did eat, Jesus said, Verily I say unto you, One of you which eateth with me shall betray me. And they began to be sorrowful, and to say unto him one by one, *Is* it I? and another *said, Is* it I? And he answered and said unto them, *It is* one of the twelve, that dippeth with me in the dish. The Son of man indeed goeth, as it is written of him: but woe to that man by whom the Son of man is betrayed! good were it for that man if he had never been born. And as they did eat, Jesus took bread, and blessed, and brake *it*, and gave to them, and said, Take, eat: this is my body. And he took the cup, and when he had given thanks, he gave *it* to them: and they all drank of it. And he said unto them, This is my blood of the new testament, which is shed for many. Verily I say unto you, I will drink no more of the fruit of the vine, until that day that I drink it new in the kingdom of God. **Mark 14:17-25**

First, we need to understand that Jesus was in a room with His disciples. These were people that He already had a relationship with. Next, we see that Jesus freely offered the wine and bread to them all. Not once did he ask them about their secret sin. He never said, "Judas, you had better not drink this cup with me because I know there is hidden sin in your life." Although Jesus *did* mention that someone in the room would betray Him, He *did not* say that this would disqualify that person from taking part in the communion.

When Judas ate the bread and drank the wine at the Last Supper he made a Covenant oath of friendship with Jesus, only to break it later by betraying Jesus in the garden. However, even at the very point of betrayal, Jesus still called Judas His friend. The Greek word "friend" used in Matthew 26:50 means "my mate and partner, my good friend". When Judas broke his Covenant with Jesus, he became a *Spiller of Salt*. You may have seen Judas spilling his salt in the famous painting of DaVinci's Last Supper, where Judas is represented as the one who overturned the container of salt.[11]

One Sunday morning, years ago, my husband Fred

and I were about to lead our church in Holy Communion. We sang several songs about the Blood of Jesus. Then Fred prayed for everyone in the room. He asked if there was anyone who wanted to receive Jesus as their Lord and Savior. He then began to talk about what Jesus did and said on the night He was betrayed. The little cups, filled to the brim, and the tiny cubes of bread were passed to everyone. All participated, except one young woman who quietly refused. I knew she was a Christian, so I was surprised that she was refusing to join us. Since we didn't want anyone to feel pressured, we quietly passed her by. She again refused to participate the next several times we celebrated Holy Communion.

I decided to ask her why she didn't join with the rest of the church. She told me she was afraid that there was secret sin in her life. What if there was something she had forgotten to confess to the Lord? Perhaps she hadn't perfectly forgiven someone. If so, she believed that she would be placing herself in great danger. Instead of being joyful, she was terrified of Holy Communion. As I began to probe her, she quickly directed me to the words of the Apostle Paul in **I Corinthians 11:27.** "Some have taken part of the Lord's Supper unworthily, and are sick, and some have even died."

> "Wherefore whosoever shall eat this bread, and drink this cup of the Lord, unworthily, shall be guilty of the body and blood of the Lord. But let a man examine himself, and so let him eat of that bread, and drink of that cup. For he that eateth and drinketh unworthily, eateth and drinketh damnation to himself, not discerning the Lord's body. For this cause many are weak and sickly among you, and many sleep." **I Corinthians 11:27-29**

I have heard many explanations concerning **I Corinthians 11:27**, but I have never understood the passage until I looked at it through the eyes of Covenant. Exactly what is the *action* that causes us to "drink damnation unto ourselves"? Is it past sin? Is it lack of respect for the cup and the bread? Or, could this action be referring to what we do *after* taking communion? Could it be repeated unfriendliness, repeated fighting and quarreling, unresolved divisions in the church, or even worse, continued unforgiveness?

The key point of confusion lies in the phrase, "not discerning the Lord's body". From the Greek we know "not discerning" means, "God forbid that we should discriminate, prefer, make judgment, withdraw from, desert, to separate in a hostile spirit, to oppose, argue with, contend with, have doubts, and disputes."[12] "Not discerning the Lord's body" means, "breaking Covenant". We also know that the "Lord's Body" is the Church, which is made up of people. The Church is not the bread and wine, the Church is you and me.[13] All of this leaves little doubt that, we "drink damnation unto ourselves" when we break Covenants with those with whom we have shared the communion supper. When we "make judgments", "argue with" and "separate in a hostile spirit", we bring a curse upon ourselves. We walk as one condemned not by someone else, but by our own mouth. A self-imposed curse is brought on our heads; some of us even die.

After communion on Sunday morning, how many people go home and criticize the choir, the youth department, or the pastor's wife? How many return home to have "roast pastor" for lunch. Communion reaffirms Covenant, not only with Christ, but with the pastor, and fellow brothers and sisters in the Church. I wonder how many people are sick, and perhaps have died, because they didn't understand the true meaning of this verse. True communion is a guaranteed oath of permanent friendship. It doesn't matter to whom the criticism is directed. For those in Covenant, criticism is "drinking damnation unto ourselves". For Covenant friends never roast their pastor for lunch.

> "Speak not evil one of another, brethren. He that speaketh evil of *his* brother, and judgeth his brother, speaketh evil of the law, and judgeth the law: but if thou judge the law, thou art not a doer of the law, but a judge." **James 4:11**

> *True communion is a guaranteed oath of permanent friendship.*

In his book *Blessing or Curse You Can Choose*, Derek Prince explains the **James 4:11** phrase, "speaking evil"[14]. Prince says that "speaking evil" is when we "speak against" fellow believers. No matter if what we say is true, **James 4:11** tells us that speaking against others in the Body of Christ is sin. Period. Prince goes on to say that when we speak evil, we also speak curses on ourselves. **James 3:6** tells us that the tongue defiles the whole body. According to Prince, "The believer who is guilty of this kind of speech [gossip, criticism, etc] actually defiles [curses] both himself and that part of the Body of Christ to which he is related."[15] As members of Jesus' Body, we must guard our tongue lest we bring curses, both upon ourselves and upon other believers.

> "Neither pray I for these alone, but for them also which shall believe on me through their word; That they all may be one; as thou, Father, art in me, and I in thee, that they also may be one in us: that the

world may believe that thou hast sent me."
John 17:20-21

Jesus prayed that we would all become one. Dr John Gills, the great scholar/historian who wrote the most detailed exposition of the scriptures that has ever been written, says that this prayer is fulfilled in the beauty of Church communion. How much more wonderful would communion be if, after reaffirming our Covenant with those in our Church body, we became **Keepers of Salt**? Salt keepers affirm vows like a bride and groom in a marriage ceremony. For richer or poorer, in sickness and health, Salt keepers commit themselves to each other. How much more lovely would we, as the Bride of Christ, become if we could embrace the beauty of true commitment in this Covenant supper?

One young woman in our church quietly refused to take communion because she thought she was "unworthy". The truth is, none of us are worthy to take communion. None of us are pure except that we are covered by the blood of Jesus. Once we have accepted Jesus as our Lord and Savior, all of our sins, for all time, have been forgiven. We have been justified. Justification is a Covenant word. *Being* justified means to be restored into a right, Covenant Friendship with Jesus Christ[16]. Eating and drinking communion with Jesus is the privilege of that friendship. We can take communion freely without fear because we are Covenant friends. In fact, we become Covenant friends with His whole body. The question is, will we move from relationship to Covenant? Will we choose to become, **Keepers of Salt**?

HIS BODY BROKEN FOR YOU

Before being led to the cross, Jesus chose to spend the last few hours of his life with His disciples at the Last Communion Supper. Of all the food Jesus and His disciples could have eaten, why did Jesus choose bread? After all, He could have cut portions of roasted meat which would have seemed a better example of His broken body. Certainly Jesus chose bread for a specific reason. The reason is very simple; the Bread Covenant.

The people of Jesus' day would often share bread as a symbol of Covenant. In fact, when bread was shared at a meal, people would recognize that they had come into a Covenant of hospitality. Covenants of hospitality were taken so seriously that the host would pledge that, for as long as the guest was in his house, he would protect him with every drop of his blood.[17] He would allow no harm to come to guests. Not only that, but the Bread Covenant also said, "Today I forgive you, I call for a truce. All past sins are forgiven and forgotten." For this reason, people were very careful about who they ate bread with. They wouldn't dare share bread with a stranger because both parties were very aware that, sharing bread meant making a Covenant.

Jesus chose bread at the Last Supper to make a Covenant with His disciples. He held the bread in His hands and told them, "This is my body." Finally, Jesus broke the bread in two, revealing to His disciples and all eternity this key Covenant principle: A Covenant is solidified when the Covenant makers demonstrate their willingness to be broken for the other.

And when he had given thanks, he brake it, and said, Take, eat: this is my body, which is broken for

you: this do in remembrance of me.
1 Corinthians 11:24

Jesus showed us what it means to be broken for one's friends. While the symbolic act of Covenant Friendship in bread breaking is a beautiful metaphor, the reality of being broken is much more sobering. For many people, self-sacrifice, laying down one's life, dying to self and humility are undesirable at best. After all, who wants to be humbled and who wants to lay down their life? It's one thing to ask for humility in word; it's quite another to willingly lay down one's life in deed.

Salt is an essential ingredient to bread. I have made many loaves of bread; every recipe that I have ever seen calls for salt. Salt is a stabilizing factor in the bread. Although salt controls the action of the yeast and other leavens, it is not itself a leaven. It strengthens the gluten, the elastic network that catches the gas produced by the yeast, enabling the bread to rise and become light. It also accents the flavor of all the other ingredients.

> *While the symbolic act of Covenant Friendship in bread breaking is a beautiful metaphor, the reality of being broken is much more sobering.*

Unleavened bread and even sodium free bread usually have small measures of salt in them. Bread made without salt is flat and tasteless. In Jesus' day, bread was the symbol of sustenance, nourishment and health. Jesus chose bread because he wanted us to know that it's our Covenant with Him that is our sustenance, nourishment and health. In fact, Jesus even said that He was "the bread" of life. It is Covenant with Jesus that brings stability to our lives and gives us strength. It is the broken bread of Covenant that makes us the "salt of the earth," allowing us to bring nourishment to others. Covenant gives our life flavor and permits us to rise above our situations. Jesus offered Himself to us as a living broken sacrifice that we could become one with Him. He willingly laid down His life that we could become like He was...broken! Will you be willing to be broken for those with whom you have come into Covenant?

> The sacrifices of God are a broken spirit: a broken and a contrite heart, O God, thou wilt not despise.
> **Psalms 51:17**

A COVENANT CHURCH

I am saddened at the lack of brotherly love, the suspicion, the backbiting, and the animosity that pervades our churches today. Jesus' death sealed a New Covenant with all believers. We read books written about this New Covenant, but we never realize that it is actually the solution to our own problems. The New Covenant is Jesus' gift of friendship, both with Him and with all believers. The New Covenant represents much more than just the remission of our sins. It is Jesus and us, joined together in the "oneness" of a Friendship Covenant. This is a friendship that refuses to backbite, that endures animosity, and lovingly believes the best in each other.

For years, I have seen people in the church enter into the communion service with fear. For them, communion is about prerequisites. Was sin confessed? All secrets exposed? Communion becomes an obligatory symbolic act with a mysterious curse attached. Fearing the curse, they search their hearts and probe for unconfessed sin. Meeting these prerequisites allows them to avoid the curse and then go about their merry Christian life. Expecting nothing more from communion, they wonder why they are not walking in all of the blessings promised to those who walk with Jesus. Some might even fear their life is "cursed"! It's time for the church to change the way it looks at the celebration of the Lord's Supper. Jesus never disqualified people with secret sin from taking part in Communion because, as **I Peter 4:8** states, the Love of Covenant Friendship "covers a multitude of sins". For believers, it's not what is done before communion that's important, it's what is done afterwards. Communion is Jesus' new Blood Covenant of friendship. It's a friendship that lives on, long after the cup and the bread

> *It's time for the church to change the way it looks at the Lord's Supper. For believers, it's not what's done before communion that's important, it's what's done afterwards.*

Is this explanation of the "New Covenant" new to you? Have you wondered what it means to take communion unworthily? Have you been afraid to participate in Holy Communion? Can you think of a time when you criticized your fellow Covenant takers? Has gossip and backbiting become the norm in your conversation? Would Jesus be ashamed of the way you treat your "friends"?

Communion is an oath; it's not just a symbol of what Jesus did for us. After taking part of the communion oath, we then must search our hearts daily. We must guard against words and deeds that betray our Blood

Covenant Friendships. When we participate in communion, we are making these oaths:

1. I now enter into Blood Covenant Friendship with You, Jesus. I am willing to lay down my life for You in the same way that You laid down Your life for me. I am willing to sacrifice all of myself, and all that I have for You because I wish to come into this Covenant Friendship. Nothing that I have is my own, but whatever I have is freely given to You. I choose to live in Covenant with You. If I break this Covenant, I recognize I will be under a self-inflicted curse.

2. I now come into Covenant with the pastor and leadership of this church. They directly represent Jesus in this solemn oath. I recognize that the pastor is the man whom I have relationship with, who guards my life as a shepherd guards the lives of his sheep. I pledge myself in Covenant, not only to Jesus, but also to my pastor. I will not hurt or cause others to hurt my pastor, because he is my Blood Covenant friend. I am in Covenant with him. If I break this Covenant, I recognize that I will be walking in a self-inflicted curse.

3. I now come into Blood Covenant Friendship with others here in this church/fellowship. I choose to be one with the body of Christ, even as Christ prayed that we all might be one. I recognize this is the Covenant prayer of my Lord, and it is my desire as well. I realize if I walk in criticism, unforgiveness, and gossip against my brother and sister, I am breaking my Covenant, and will be walking in a self-inflicted curse.

The world often laughs and pokes fun at the Church. We call it persecution. The Devil calls it strategy. The truth is, the Devil has blinded our eyes so that the world sees what we don't. The world sees an ineffective Church, persecuting *itself* through curses of their own broken Covenants. Jesus did not want the Covenant of communion to defile us. His desire was for blessings, not curses. His desire was for a church full of friends, not just pew partners. He made himself a self-surrendered blood sacrifice for the sake of friendship. [18] His Covenant Friendship endured all, even His own death, as He gave us the greatest blessing of all. Will you embrace His friendship?

Will you be a **Keeper of Salt**?

> *The New Covenant is Jesus' gift of friendship, both with Him and with all believers. The New Covenant is much more than just the remission of our sins. It's Jesus and us, joined together in the "oneness" of a Friendship Covenant.*

NOTES:

To have a good friend is one of the highest delights of life; to be a good friend is one of the noblest and most difficult undertakings.

— Anonymous

CHAPTER 3

YOU CAN'T OFFEND ME

Have you ever had a friend who seems to stick with you no matter what happens? No matter if you lose your temper or let a hurtful word slip, this friend just doesn't seem to care. It's not that they're not listening; rather, this is a sign of a friendship that has moved from mere relationship to Covenant. Most people only have a few friends who truly understand Covenant and who are willing to pay the price for this kind of wonderful friendship. True Covenant friends say, "You can't offend me."

Growing up, I was blessed with wonderful relationships with my mother, grandmothers and sister. However, once I married and the Lord began to move me out of my comfort zone, miles away from those relationships, I realized I needed other friendships. I spent several lonely years as a pastor's wife. I wanted friendships, but another pastor's wife had told me that I shouldn't have friends in the church. I needed to keep a "professional distance" because "friends" would not respect my ministry. Through painful experiences, I found that her advice *seemed* to be true.

These experiences only served to reinforce my fear of deep friendship within the church. I had seen so many people offended with their pastor over petty issues that, in the light of eternity, were inconsequential. I had even seen churches fall apart because of a few hurt feelings. I knew in my heart there had to be more to church relationships than my experiences has taught me. Surely I wasn't the only one who longed for Covenant relationships that could withstand trivial offenses. Nevertheless, my experience told me that friendship was something I needed to sacrifice for the sake of ministry.

Peggy and her husband David had moved to our town and visited the church where Fred and I pastored. I felt a special connection to Peggy the first time I saw her and hoped they would come again, but they didn't. The Lord had directed them to attend another church. Yet, I couldn't ignore the desire to get to know Peggy better. Sunday after Sunday I would sit on the piano bench, which had a great view of the back door, and look for her to come. I remember praying, "Lord, please bring Peggy back here." Now I certainly wasn't about to "steal" them from another church. In fact, I never even asked Peggy and David to come to our church. Yet, Somehow I knew in my heart that Peggy and I would be friends. I wanted her to come, so I looked and prayed. Finally, a few years later, the Lord directed Peggy and David to our church. This time they stayed. I was thrilled, for I knew at that moment that my prayers had been answered.

As good friends do, Peggy and I went on shopping

trips and school outings. Although we did many things together, the time we spent praying together was the most memorable. We prayed for our husbands, our children and for others in the church. We even prayed for people we didn't know! One of the lessons I learned from my relationship with Peggy was that the time you spend in prayer with someone is the cement that glues your Covenant friendship together.

Peggy and David have two children, Kate and Billy. Billy was about four years old when he developed a love for guitars. My husband Fred and Peggy's husband David both played guitar in church and, as you might imagine, Billy wanted to play too. Billy was so cute the first Sunday when he came to church with his guitar. He really didn't make much noise and most people didn't seem to mind the fact that Billy had not a clue of how to play a guitar. Everyone in the church began to enjoy Billy's "playing" so much that, after a few Sundays, some were watching Billy in place of worshiping the Lord.

Fred came to me one Sunday morning and said, "We need to talk to David and Peg about Billy playing his guitar in church. He is just too cute and his guitar playing is distracting. Either you talk to them or I will." My heart sank into my chest and I thought it would break. It seemed to me that every time Fred and I would speak to people about their children, they would take personal offense and soon after leave the church. I just knew that this would be the offense that would end my friendship with Peggy and I feared that she and her family would leave the church. I didn't want to disappoint Billy, and I definitely didn't want to lose my new friend. But Fred was right; the guitar had to go.

Peg and I were scheduled to supervise junior church that Sunday morning. I entered the children's room and sat down in a tiny chair meant for children. With my feet propped up on another tiny chair, I put my hands over my face and started to cry. Peggy was immediately concerned because I'm not usually a tearful person. So she asked me what was wrong.

"You're going to leave the church!" my fearful heart blurted.

Peggy was surprised at such a strange statement and with a puzzled look on her face asked, "Why?"

"Billy can't play guitar in the church anymore and now you're going to leave."

I'll never forget the look of shock on Peg's face as she said, "Debby, my love for you and Pastor Fred is not dependant on whether Billy can play guitar or not. This isn't a problem. We won't leave the church."

> *Covenant friends stay when everyone else walks away. They see all situations through the eyes of Covenant.*

It was at that moment, with tears in my eyes, that I realized that Peggy was a Covenant friend, a friend who would not be offended. Even today, over fifteen years later, this story still brings tears to my eyes. Peggy's response demonstrated to me that she was a **Keeper of Salt**!

Peggy and David never did leave the church until they moved out of the state. They have continued to be very dear friends. Miles cannot separate Covenant and neither can time, but best of all, neither can offense.

In **John 6** Jesus taught some very hard things that rubbed a lot of people the wrong way. After He was finished speaking, many of His followers left Him. He then turned to His closest disciples and asked them if they would leave too. Jesus was looking to see if they, too were offended. He wanted to see if their *commitment* to Him was stronger than *offense*.

Peter answered, "No, we won't go. Where else could we go? You alone have the words of eternal life."

Peter didn't let the hard words of Jesus strain their friendship. Peter could not be offended because of a choice he had already made. It was a Covenant between Peter and Jesus that compelled Peter to set his eyes on eternal life, a gaze so fixed that Jesus would later call him "a rock". It was Covenant that drew Peter into closer relationship when others retreated in offense.

Those in Covenant friendships are willing to pay the price often required to keep relationships intact. Covenant friends stay when everyone else walks away. They see all situations through the eyes of Covenant. They look at people and see what no one else sees, a relationship that is worth dying for, a prize greater than any offense.

At this point let me give you a word of caution: We should never "take advantage" of Covenant to purposely offend someone. For example, I know a man who actually uses offense as a technique. When he suspects disloyalty from someone under his leadership, he purposely offends that person and then observes their reaction. If that person uses the offense as an excuse to leave, he knows that a Covenant relationship never really existed. If the person stays and is not offended, then the he knows he has someone very loyal.

THE SIN OF OFFENSE

Rev. Carlton Spencer (a former president of Elim Bible Institute in Lima, New York) often said, "**It is as much a sin to be offended as it is to offend**." Many times we think that the offender is the only one at fault. However, if you take offense and give it a home in your heart, water it with a good dose of bitterness and unforgiveness, you are also at fault. Love, in **1 Corinthians 13**, is not easily offended. Love isn't easily angered and doesn't keep a record of wrongs. Love is kind and gentle. None of these characteristics fit well with offense. Forgiveness dictates that we must lay down our right to be hurt. Instead, we must believe the best in others and repay offense with love.

Marriage vows often include, "for better or for worse, for richer or for poorer, in sickness and in health. Here I pledge you my faith". In essence, the marriage vow means: "No matter what you do or become, no matter what the situation that may occur, nothing shall offend me. I no longer have the right to be offended. I give you my faith. I understand that faith is not faith until it has been tried, and it has not been tried until it has been offended and still remains faithful. When something happens that could offend me, I will choose to not take offense. And by all this, I will prove my faith."

I don't want to lay a guilt trip on anyone who has

taken the marriage pledge, and for one reason or another, broke the Covenant. However, it is important that we see that the marriage Covenant explicitly states that, "I realize there will be opportunities for offense in our marriage, but I will choose not to be offended". Of course we don't expect that the person we marry will hurt us on purpose, but couples often experience offenses. In relationships, our most private life is exposed, thus making us vulnerable. It takes a great deal of trust to completely "let down our guard" and give up the right to be offended.

Covenant is not just about marriage; it's about any relationship where two people have agreed to walk together. Siblings fight in every family, but they learn to get along. In the Body of Christ we have many brothers and sisters, supplying us with ample opportunities for disagreements and offense. We too must learn to get along. However, while brothers and sisters may choose to eventually separate, those in Covenant cannot. We must not break our Covenants or even minimize our promises. Instead, we must choose to not be offended so that the work of the Lord will reach its full accomplishment.[1] I have seen the consequences to those who allow themselves to become offended and then remain in unforgiveness. Offense walks hand in hand with unforgiveness, and together these two share a lonely life. I was lonely until I found a friend who would not be offended. Now we walk in Covenant and enjoy the blessing that Covenant relationships provide.

Go ahead. Take the risk of making Covenant friendships. If you sow offense-free friendship, you will reap offense-free friendship. Once you've made a Covenant friend, be forgiving and don't allow yourself to become offended. Be willing to walk in Covenant and you will enjoy the blessings of Covenant for the rest of your life. You will then be a **Keeper of Salt**!

Love is kind and gentle. None of these characteristics fit well with offense. Forgiveness dictates that we must lay down our right to be hurt. Instead, we must believe the best in others and repay offense with love.

NOTES:

A friend is someone who understands your past, believes in your future, and accepts you today just the way you are.

Cruel is the strife of brothers.

— Aristotle

CHAPTER 4

COVENANT BREAKERS (THE SPILLING OF SALT)

Abby and her family began attending our church, when our families soon became friends. They often ate at our house, sometimes several times a week. We shared our dreams and sorrows. I prayed with her and she with me. There were days we spent working on the old church building, and of course we went shopping! I thought we had a good relationship. I thought we were friends. I thought we were Covenant friends.

Then one Sunday morning a few years later, Abby and her family didn't come to church. I wondered why because they had just been to our house for dinner the night before, and Abby didn't say they wouldn't be in church. I wondered if someone in her family was sick. I also thought it was strange since they hadn't been to church the Sunday before either. But, after all, it was

Christmas time and people were often busy. I asked another woman in the church if she knew why Abby and her family were absent. To my surprise, she told me that Abby and her husband had decided to attend another church. They weren't coming to our church anymore!

I was shocked. No, stunned speechless was more like it! Abby never said anything to me about leaving the church. I was not prepared for this information. I was hurt, but that wasn't the end of my sorrow. I later found out that Abby had been openly critical of Fred and I for several months leading up to their leaving our church. As a result of their criticism, some others in the church left as well. I felt betrayed and, yes I was offended. How could a "friend" do this to me? I prayed and hoped that God would somehow make it all right.

One day God spoke to me and said, "If you want to be healed in your heart, pray for Abby."

Pray for Abby? Why would I want to do that? She hurt me. Even if I did pray, what would I say? Oh God, please punish this woman, my former friend! That would be easy. I thought, surely God would judge anyone who had hurt me that much. But somehow that didn't seem right. How should I pray? What was God really asking me to do?

Then He said, "Pray that Abby receives from *Me*, the same blessings that you want for *yourself*."

I said, "Oh God that's hard. I want to pray that you'll judge her. I want revenge to satisfy my bruised heart. She has hurt me too much."

But God said, "If you want to be healed in your heart, pray a blessing on her."

So, for two years I prayed and blessed Abby. When driving past her house, I would bless her. I would pray and pray and pray again. It became my goal to pray for her every day, even though I didn't want to. I wanted God to judge her, not bless her. But I wanted what God wanted more.

I didn't know that my heart was being healed until after I attended a weekend conference. I returned home tired, but excited about the wonderful things God had done in my life. The next morning I had a strong desire to call Abby. It had been two years since I had spoken to her. Never once in those two years did I have the desire to call her or speak to her. If God had asked me to call the week before, I think I would have been scared and re-sistant. But on this morning God didn't need to ask me to call her; I wanted to. That morning I began to see Abby, not as an enemy, but as a child of God whom He wanted to bless. I didn't see her the same way I did before because sud-denly, I began to see Abby through the eyes of Covenant. Now I wanted to talk to her, so I picked up the phone and called.

> *My part of the Covenant was to go after the one with whom I had Covenanted.*

When Abby answered the phone, I could tell that she was just as surprised to hear from me as I was to call! Before long, she began to share about some difficult fam-ily situations. She had been praying for someone to call and pray with her. Had the Lord not healed my heart, I could have never prayed a prayer of faith with her. Now, after two years of bitter silence, I was on the phone praying with her. It was wonderful!

What amazed me the most was that for those two years, I thought Abby was the Covenant breaker. It never occurred to me that I had broken Covenant as well. You see, I never made an effort to contact her until after the Lord healed my heart. I didn't even try. I blamed the broken relationship on her since she was the one who I thought had done the offending and the breaking away. I never realized that my part of the Covenant was to go after the one with whom I had Covenanted. I wallowed in my self-pity and sorrow, allowing the years to deepen the gap. It wasn't until God did a work in me that I called her. Did she do wrong? Yes. But was I also a Covenant breaker? Yes! We were both Covenant breakers. I now see my *responsibility* as a **Keeper of Salt** is to be someone who does everything I can to keep the Covenant going. Neglecting that responsibility is itself a violation of Covenant.

Jesus taught us the parable of the Good Shepherd in **Matthew 18:12**. The parable goes something like this: If a shepherd has a hundred sheep and one of them runs away, he will surely leave the ninety-nine just to go looking for the one lost sheep.

In other words, the shepherd doesn't say, "I can't believe that sheep, after all I have done for him. He has really hurt me leaving like that. What is wrong with that lamb anyway? I have done so much for him. I have loved him, fed him and cleaned up after him. He didn't even say good-bye. This really hurts! Well he is gone now; I guess I'll have to get over this rejection. I just can't believe he would do this. I am so hurt. From now on I will never trust any of these other sheep again. After all, they were all in on this. They all knew this would happen, and none of them even bothered to tell me."

No, the Good Shepherd doesn't say these things. Instead he goes out and looks for the lost one. Like the shepherd, I wasn't the one who originally broke the Covenant friendship. However, I was in no mood to go look for my lost friend. I was much too busy licking my

> *God is not as interested in the fact that you were offended as He is interested in how you will react to the offense.*

wounds and spilling the salt of our friendship. I was so distracted by the problems in other's lives that I almost missed the Word of the Lord in my own life. It wasn't until God spoke to me to pray for my friend that I began to look beyond what she had done.

I am so glad I allowed the Lord to work on my heart. If I hadn't, I have no idea what the bitterness would have done to me. Bitterness is a wicked thing; it erodes the heart and dulls our sensitivity to the Lord[1]. The Lord changed my whole attitude about Abby while I was praying for her. Little by little my heart was healed. The pain was not as intense, and the bitterness just disappeared. When I began to see through Covenant eyes, I didn't see her as the enemy anymore. I saw her the way Jesus saw her. I wouldn't say our relationship is the same as it was; perhaps it will never be the same. Since that day on the phone though, we have had other occasions to talk and pray for each other. Our relationship has been mended in many ways. I wonder how much stronger our friendship would be today had I pursued her years ago. I have resolved that from now on, if someone leaves me, I will run after them.

WALLS OF BROKEN TRUST

We often close our hearts after we have been hurt. I have watched wounded people slowly close their hearts to others, then eventually close their heart to God. We do this when we build up walls to protect us from future hurt, to insulate us from emotional pain, and to isolate us from those we fear. However, we often don't realize that walls around our heart shut out those we love, including God. Then we wonder what has happened to the presence of the Lord.

When Abby left the church, I responded by withdrawing. Instead of pursuing the relationship, I chose to build a wall. As a result, I found that my relationship with the Lord could only go so far. The Lord would bump into my wall, and then I would sense Him withdrawing. As soon as I would begin to heal from the hurt, someone would bring up the subject of Abby leaving the church, and my wall would go up once again.

It wasn't long before I began to close myself off to many women in the church who wanted to be my friend. I didn't trust anyone. I remember one day when a very sweet woman in the church wanted to come to see me. She made an evening appointment. I did everything I could to change the appointment because I was scared. My imagination went wild with thoughts of the many ways she could hurt me. I struggled all day thinking that in the evening when she arrived, she would cut me up in little pieces with her words. I had never been afraid of anyone like this before, and I was shocked at myself. This woman was known for being sweet and gentle, yet my closed heart had caused me to be warped in my thinking. I didn't feel the peace of God anymore. The only thing I could feel was the pride of my own self preservation.

How foolish I felt, after the evening was over, and the woman had gone home. All she had wanted to do was reaffirm her love for me. I had thought the worst, while she had thought the best. I began to realize that I couldn't live like this. I couldn't be so suspicious of people. I had to give them a chance. I had to open up, be a Covenant person, and give them opportunity to hurt me. I had to believe that God is the mender of broken hearts and a rewarder of those who love.[2]

As I drew closer to the Lord, He required me to tear down pieces of my walls. As He worked in my life, I slowly began to trust people again. It wasn't easy, and it didn't happen overnight. It took over two years. But it was worth it. I learned about forgiveness and trust. I learned that when we are in Covenant, we sometimes get hurt. And I learned that, being hurt is okay. Jesus was hurt by those He was closest to, yet He still went to the cross for them. For those in Covenant, hurt is not an excuse for unforgivness or bitterness.

LONILINESS, THE CONSEQUENCE OF BROKEN COVENANTS

I have seen many people suffer and struggle in church. The feelings of loneliness overwhelm them. Yet we know that Jesus was touched in the same way as we are.[3] He suffered for us so we wouldn't have to. One of the key plans of the devil is to make us think we are alone and that no one cares or understands us. So often we believe that we are the only one in the world with our specific problem. We don't believe that anyone, much less Jesus, can understand how we feel. The Bible does say, that Jesus was tempted like us, but let's get real; Jesus was never a woman!

Once a woman said to me, "I feel like I'm the only one in the church with an unsaved husband. I just don't fit here anymore. I'm wondering if I should still come to church, or go some place else."

Then another said, "I feel like I'm the only one in the church who is a widow. I just don't fit here any more."

> *Jesus knew what it felt like to have people betray Covenant. Jesus did know how I feel, but unlike me, Jesus did not build walls to isolate Himself.*

Another came and said, "My children don't serve the Lord, and I am the only one in the church with my situation. I don't belong."

Several others came too, and the story was the same, "I am the only one."

Then I realized that I too thought I was "the only one". I had often said to the Lord, "I am the only pastor's wife in the church. No one understands me. I am alone, and I just don't fit in with anyone else." What a shock it was for me to hear the heart-cry of so many others, saying out loud what I had been feeling in my heart for so long. I asked the Lord, "What is the problem with all of us?

We all feel like we are the only one in the church with our problem."

The Lord revealed something that I will never forget. He showed me that hurt feels the same to everyone. We know that Jesus suffered the greatest pain imaginable. The Lord helped me to understand that the pain in my heart and body feels the same as it did to Jesus when He was on this earth. Yes, He truly did know how I feel. He knew what it was like to feel alone and have His own Father forsake Him. He felt rejected and forgotten, abused and humiliated.[4] Jesus knew what it felt like to have people betray Covenant. Jesus **did** know how I feel, but unlike me, Jesus did not build walls to isolate Himself. The Lord revealed to me that the walls we build to protect ourselves, actually blind us to comfort from those on the other side who are feeling the same pain as we do. We can't even experience Jesus' empathy for us until we bring down the wall of self preservation and allow His grace to touch us. No, I wasn't the only one and neither are you. Jesus truly knows how you feel, even if you are a woman!

Have you been hurt? Have relationships left you disappointed? Do you look at people with suspicious eyes, wondering if you can trust them? Have people broken their Covenants with you? Are you courageous enough to look past your pain and let God heal you? If you are at these crossroads and if you want to experience the power of Covenant in your own life, then take these next four steps to heart.

First, realize that you aren't the only one who has felt the pain of a broken Covenant. Thinking "I am the only one" is a very effective plot of the enemy. It closes us off from others, and keeps us from making and honoring Covenants. God knows exactly how you feel. The Bible is full of examples of broken Covenants with God. Also remember that "pain is pain" for everyone. Although others may not be in the exact same predicament as you, they can still relate to your grief as they can identify with your hurt.

Next, don't close your heart. Don't build up a wall that keeps everyone out. If you have built a wall, take a chance and remove a few bricks. The Lord will help you if you ask Him. Allow yourself to trust again. Experience the invigorating freedom that comes when Jesus heals your heart. Allow yourself to rest in the safety of a renewed Covenant.

Don't let others determine what you do. Don't let bitterness swindle you into becoming a Covenant breaker yourself. This is the biggest temptation of all, to retaliate once you have been hurt. We have all been hurt and we have all been offended. God is not as interested in the fact that you were offended as much as He is interested in how you will react to the offense. Those who seek revenge are the same as those who break Covenant. Don't give in. Be a **Keeper of Salt!**

Finally, don't give up. I can't guarantee that every Covenant relationship will be restored right away, or that it ever will be restored. There have been those with whom my husband and I have tried for years to restore relationship, yet they continue to resist our attempts. We continue to pursue restoration though, believing that someday we will see our Covenant friendships repaired. Don't give in to hopelessness. Hopelessness deteriorates faith, destroys trust and builds walls. God is faithful and

He keeps His Covenant. Don't give up. Be a **Keeper of Salt!**

> And let us not be weary in well doing: for in due season we shall reap, if we faint not. **Galatians 6:9**

> *Don't let others determine what you do. Don't let bitterness swindle you into becoming a Covenant breaker yourself.*

Those who expect to reap the blessings of freedom must undergo the fatigue of supporting it.

— Thomas Paine

CHAPTER 5

THINGS TOO WONDERFUL

One day a few years ago, I heard the Lord ask, "What do you think would happen if American Christians spent as much time praying for their President, as they did criticizing him?" I began to think, what *would* happen? Of course we have had some Presidents who have been more Christ-like than others. However, I'm always amazed by the amount of criticism that I hear from Christians against any person in leadership. So often it seems that we don't pray for people simply because we don't like them or because they hurt us. Then if we *do* pray, we pray that God would judge them. Just as when the Lord asked me to pray for my friend Abby, so often we pray for a curse instead of a blessing. People who offend us become our enemy. Our pride begins to puff up as we believe that "we are on God's side" and that we are "right". Now it is God's responsibility to "smite" our enemy, thereby lifting us up to the lofty place that we think we deserve. We will call this type of behavior the "smite my offender" syndrome.

The Bible contains many examples of the "smite my offender" syndrome. Jonah experienced this in his dealings with the people of Nineveh. Jonah didn't like it very much when God in His mercy forgave the Ninevites.[1] Jonah relished the fact that these people were sinners and that God would judge them. Or, take for example James and John. They wanted God to rain down fire on a Samaritan town because the people there had rejected Jesus. Yet, Jesus told them that they didn't know what kind of spirit was influencing them.[2] Like Jonah, James and John, too often we also find ourselves wanting to see God judge people solely to prove that we are "right". It's pride, plain and simple. We want God to disgrace them for their sin, and exalt us for our righteousness. Jesus cautioned us that, when we take on this mindset, we don't know what kind of a spirit by which we are influenced. **James 1:20** says that the *violence* of men does not work the righteousness of God. I would like to suggest that, neither does the *criticism* of men.

I recently heard Ted Haggard, President of the National Association of Evangelicals, speak at a pastors' conference. I was delighted to hear his opinion on some recent decisions made by the President of the United States. Haggard simply stated, "These things are too wonderful for me." He went on to explain that the President has information that the rest of the people in the United States may not know about. He has counsel that they will never hear and he has resources they will never employ. Therefore, according to Haggard, neither he nor the average American has a right to sit in judgment.

CRITICIZM, THE ENEMY OF COVENANT

We know from **Daniel 2:21** that the Lord deter-
mines "the course of world events", and "removes kings
and sets others on the throne". Further, we know from
Titus 3:2 that we are not to "speak evil" of any man, including people of authority.[3] Now, you may agree that
the Lord has appointed those in leadership over you, and
you may also agree that we are not to "speak evil" against
them. But, you may ask, what does this have to do with
Covenant? You might say, "I don't remember ever making a Covenant with my government leaders, especially
the President! What about freedom of speech? Isn't it
my *right* to criticize the government?" When it comes to
criticism, freedom of speech is not unlike God's gift of
free will. Yes, you have freedom to criticize your governmental leaders, and yes, you have free will to live a life of
sin and damn yourself to
hell. Notwithstanding,
it is essential to under-
stand that there are dif-
ferent ways by which
we can come into Cove-
nants. For example, there are some Covenants which God
has instituted over us beyond our will. A son is bound
under a God-instituted covenant with his father. Sons do
not choose their fathers, God does. Although sonship is
involuntary, that certainly does not exclude a son from the
bonds of Covenant. Sons are bound by the Biblical man-
date to "honor [their] father and mother", implicitly,
"whether they would choose them or not".[4] Or, as another example, believers come into Covenant with Christ
when they declare themselves to be a "believer", "a fol-
lower of Christ", or "a Christian". Finally, those who call
themselves "Americans" come into Covenant with Amer-

> *Those in Covenant cannot
> criticize each other: they are
> obligated to bless each other.*

ica. Citizenship is voluntary; therefore people can ultimately reject their citizenship and move to another country anytime they choose. Nonetheless, if they choose to remain, they *voluntarily* choose to accept both the *privileges* and the *obligations* of citizenship. They choose to be bound in a Covenant with the Constitution, the laws of the land and with the governmental leaders. To reiterate, we *don't* have the right to criticize governmental leaders, including the President, because we have voluntarily chosen to be in Covenant with them. Those in Covenant cannot criticize each other; they are obligated to bless each other.

Just as many people criticize their governmental leaders, they also criticize the leaders within their church. Sometimes their criticism becomes so prolific that they put on critical glasses. They begin to criticize everything they see. They put on a garment of criticism instead of a garment of righteousness. Sometimes after years of criticism, there is no faith left to believe God for a miracle! When people become critical, a vicious cycle of condemnation and bitterness begins. It is hard to see change even when change happens. It is easier to see problems and seemingly impossible situations, instead of walking in faith, trusting God for a miraculous change.

> *When people become critical, a vicious cycle of criticism and bitterness begins. It is hard to see change even when change happens.*

We must not forget that we serve a God of the impossible, and that He specializes in things that are impossible![5] If God saved many of our current world leaders, some Christians wouldn't believe it. Sure, they believe with their lips that "God can save anyone", but their hearts lack the faith to be truly convinced. They find it suspicious whenever anyone of notoriety comes to know the Lord. This is the same lack of faith we see in the early Christians of the Apostle Paul's day. Before Paul was saved, he was a notorious man intent on killing many Christians. After he met the Lord, it was hard for people to believe and trust Paul.[6] True, they believed that God *could* save him, but they didn't think that God actually would.

Certainly the people of Paul's day had good reason to be incredulous. However, there is a fine line between being incredulous and losing faith. Not knowing the hearts of the people of Paul's day, it is impossible to know if they truly lost faith. But imagine this scenario: They didn't know God's plans. They didn't have God's wisdom. They didn't have God's perspective, and they certainly didn't know that God would appear up to Paul with a blinding light. Not knowing things that were "too wonderful for them", they took matters into their own hands. They gave up hope, they gave up prayer and they resolved to criticism. They cursed Paul for his persecu-

> *Lost faith in God is criticism of God.*

tion. Did they break Covenant with Paul? No, they broke Covenant with God. They lost their faith. Lost faith *in* God is criticism *of* God. God's plans are much too wonderful for us and we don't have the right to stop trusting Him. We don't have the right to criticize his creation. We don't have the right to lose faith in Him. As part of our Covenant *with* God, we are obligated to have faith *in* God.

INDEPENDENCE THE ENEMY OF COVENANT

As U.S. citizens, we pride ourselves in our independence. We love and cherish our freedom, and rightly so. However our independence doesn't work without Covenant. Each State in the United States has a Covenant with the Federal Government. The country works together as one body functioning in separate states. Yet the Covenant is not hailed as the important aspect of American government. Freedom is. Americans sing about freedom, and learn about freedom. Sadly though, the American culture has forgotten Covenant.

Although I love my freedom, I have come to realize that the spirit of freedom and independence can sometimes become the enemy of Covenant. The spirit of independence has poured into our churches, organizations, and family life. We are independent from our church, so we leave and badmouth the pastor on the way out. We are independent from our family, so we divorce our spouses and neglect our children. (This is true both in America and worldwide.) We have the attitude that we don't need anyone, and we don't want anyone. Because of independence, we not only have lost respect for authority, we neither understand nor practice submission.[7] *Dependence* has become a bad word, directly connected with weakness and vulnerability.

Many churches have also succumbed to the spirit of independence. Members lack respect for church leadership, while the church leadership has little desire to recognize their need for their flock. No one wants to *need* someone else. Many have adopted the motto, "It's my way or the highway." As a result, they have given birth to what my husband Fred calls *Kangaroo Christians*. These type of people "hop" from church to church, never coming into Covenant with anyone. They say, "I don't have to stay any place, or in any church if I don't want to, because I am independent. I don't need anyone." Sadly, church hopping has become the norm in America. Instead of churches growing because of new members, they grow because people left another church. Again, because Covenant is lost, soon these people will again "hop" to another church and the story goes on.

Consider the story of David and Saul. It is interesting that even though King Saul sought to kill David, David wouldn't touch King Saul. David honored the Covenant that God had made with Saul. David couldn't even touch Saul's garments without much grief and conviction.[8] David understood the importance of Covenant. David understood that it was God who placed Saul in the kingship position, and that God was in control of the leadership of Israel. Often, because we think we know better or we think we have the right information, we sit in judgment of our leaders allowing ourselves to become frustrated. [9]

When Fred and I were first married, we attended a church in Virginia. We really enjoyed the people, but it was difficult for me to not be involved in all of the details of the church. You see, growing up as a pastor's daughter, I was used to being informed of all the inner-working details of the church. I felt left out. I didn't realize that the Lord was testing me.

We became a part of the young adult's group. One day, the pastor informed us that a certain young man was going to head up the group. I was surprised, because I didn't feel he had the qualities or maturity to do the job. I even told the pastor my opinion. Yes, I knew God *could* use this young man, but I didn't think he was a good choice. I couldn't understand why the pastor didn't also see this young man's inadequacies. Instead, the pastor just smiled at me and said he had made his decision. It was then that I understood, it wasn't any of my business! I wish I could have heard Ted Haggard way back then. These things were too wonderful for me! I was complaining about a situation that I didn't truly understand. I didn't know the reasoning behind the pastor's selection. It wasn't my place *to* understand. I wasn't the pastor, and it really wasn't any of my business. My business was to support the pastor and the person he put in charge of the young adult's group. I was obligated by Covenant to my church, to the pastor of my church, and therefore to the leaders that my pastor appointed. In fact, I had a responsibility to pray for the success of this young man's ministry.

Let's look at the story of Absalom, David's son. Absalom broke Covenant with his father David by speaking of things that were "too wonderful" for him. Absalom sat at the gate of the city; whenever someone entered with a question or criticism for the king, Absalom had a people-pleasing answer. He knew just what to say, as he offered his opinions freely. Day after day he would undermine the authority of his father by discussing things that were none of his business. He rejected his Covenant relationship with the king in an attempt to take the kingdom. It was pride that deceived him into thinking that he could. After all, he was handsome and smart. He had many wonderful opinions and would make a great king, or so he thought. But his broken Covenant brought about a war in the kingdom. In the end, Absalom's broken Covenant led to his own death.

TRUST, THE FRIEND OF COVENANT

Once, when my husband and I were pastoring, we came under a lot of criticism because of a decision we had made about counseling a couple who were having severe marital problems. Several people in the church felt we were wrong, that we were not willing to counsel the struggling couple. What they didn't know was that we tried to counsel the couple, but the wife had told Fred that she was afraid of her husband. She said that if Fred persisted in trying to counsel them, she feared she would suffer unpleasant consequences. She asked Fred not to come to their house, and she wouldn't answer the door if he did. We couldn't tell everyone about the private conversation Fred had had. It really wasn't anyone else's business. These personal details were certainly "too wonderful" for others in the church.

Pastoring a church in a small community wasn't always easy for Fred and I. There never seemed to be enough people to do all the tasks. Children's church and nursery were often the first places to suffer. When our church was new, we were always looking for volunteers. Young mothers were overjoyed when some of the teenagers in the church volunteered to take care of their children during the morning service. What most people didn't know was that Fred and I had information about a certain young man who posed a threat to the welfare of the children. As a result of this information, we made a rule: "No teenagers in the children's ministry". The information we had was not public, and we legally couldn't offer any explanation for our "no teen" rule. One young mother who was frustrated with this new rule called us. She knew that this particular young man had volunteered, and she was excited that someone was willing to help take care of her children. After all, the young man was from a Christian family, and he really liked children. That was the problem. He *liked* children! We were not about to let him work in our youth department. Fred told her that he was sorry, but that he had to enforce the rule. She hung up the phone, a little upset, but after a while she called back and apologized. God had spoken to her, so she decided to trust us. If we said no, there must be a good reason. She would pray that the Lord would provide another way. She chose to walk with us in Covenant, and trust God in this situation. She was a **Keeper of Salt!**

Well-intentioned people, offering advice that was none of their business, have destroyed many churches. These people think they are wise, when in reality they are very foolish. There are also those people who decide to walk in a Covenant of trust. These people always believe the best, even when they don't know all of the facts. However, they also realize that Covenant is much more than blind submission. It is a willingness to work together, pray together and trust each other.

I have learned that there are a lot of things that are "too wonderful" for me. I am also learning that I don't have to know everything. Trust is a learned gift. When we trust, we are telling God, "I have confidence because You are in control. You are working out all things in my life for my good."[10]

> *Covenant is much more than blind submission. It is a willingness to work together, pray together, and trust each other.*

Trusting gives us peace. We don't have to worry about things that are "too wonderful" for us. Many things just aren't any of our business. If we don't understand something, we can pray and trust God to work it out. Then when we are finished with our prayer, we must determine to leave things in God's hands. If there *is* something we can do to fix the situation, then God will tell us. If the Lord doesn't say anything, maybe it's "too wonderful." In that case we should leave the situation with Him!

One of the blessings of Covenant is peace. If I trust, I will be blessed with peace, knowing that God will honor my Covenant. Even if a friend is wrong, my pastor is wrong, or the President of the United States is wrong, God will honor me if I am faithful to my Covenant with them. Perhaps when I get to heaven I will find out that it was *me* who was wrong. Perhaps there are things I don't know, that all these things were "too wonderful" for me!

I choose to be a **Keeper of Salt**!

Love is an image of God, and not a lifeless image, but the living essence of the all divine nature which beams full of all goodness.

— Martin Luther

CHAPTER 6

COVENANT MAKERS

Sandy approached me one Sunday as we were leaving church. She told me that she was having a lot of difficulties at work and in her family. I asked her if she would like me to pray with her, and she said yes. After we prayed, I suggested that she find someone to pray with her on a regular basis. She needed someone who would comfort her and not betray her confidence. However, Sandy explained that because of her work and family schedule, it would be difficult for her to have a regular prayer time with anyone. I suggested that she and I try to work out a time. The only time we could arrange was 5:00 o'clock on Thursday mornings. My flesh didn't really like the idea of this early morning commitment, but in my heart I knew it was the right thing to do. So, for over two years, Sandy and I met Thursday mornings at 5:00AM.

Some Covenants we make are only for a season. The Covenant you make with the local department store each time you purchase an item is a seasonal Covenant. Most stores guarantee their products for thirty or ninety days. The Covenant made with a bakery for a wedding cake is just for a season, until the day of the wedding. The Covenant I made to pray with Sandy was not for the rest of our lives, but for a season.

I discovered that Sandy had a unique ability to pray and reach the heart of God. She was sincere, and wholly devoted to the Lord, even though her life had many frustrations. I also discovered that she wasn't interested in praying only for herself, but for my needs as well. She never asked questions that would compromise my position as the pastor's wife. She was a Covenant intercessor.

Although I don't know all that happened in the Spirit realm when Sandy and I prayed, I do know that I was changed by the experience. It wasn't until Fred and I left to be missionaries to Russia that Sandy and I stopped praying together. I have seen her on a few occasions since then, and whenever I do, I feel an unusual connection. I can still sense a spiritual bond between us.

Something wonderful happens when we make a Covenant. It is the invisible glue that binds us together. You can't see it, but you can feel it. For example, if you make a purchase at a department store and then return the item, and if the department store honors their return commitment, then you will be inclined to buy from them again. It might even become your favorite store. Or, if you order a cake from a bakery, and if the cake is wonderful, this baker will have earned your trust. You will suggest this bakery to your friends, and it will probably become your favorite bakery. On the other hand, if the cake is bad, you may never use this bakery again. If I had told Sandy that I would pray with her on Thursday mornings, then after a month or so decided that I didn't want to get up so early in the morning anymore, she would have understood, although someplace in her heart she would have felt that I didn't really care, and that she wasn't worth my effort. Nonetheless, I *did* care. She *was* worth my effort, so we continued to meet at 5:00AM. We both kept the Covenant discovering that the by-product of a successful Covenant is an invisible glue that makes our relationships strong.

> *Covenant prayer is one of the strongest and most effective ways of making friendships.*

Covenant prayer is one of the strongest and most effective ways of making friendships. I am so glad I spent those two years praying with Sandy. I have wonderful memories of those times. We didn't spend our time talking; we just sipped our first coffee of the day and prayed. As a result we saw God change peoples' lives. We saw situations turn around. We saw our lives become more effective. We found out first-hand that Covenant prayer is effective. We saw the reality of Jesus' words in **Matthew 18:19** when He said, "Again I say unto you, that if two of you shall agree on earth as touching anything that they shall ask, it shall be done for them of my Father which is in heaven." No wonder Jesus said if two or more are gathered in His name He would be in the midst [1]. Gathering in Covenant prayer is a reflection of who *He* is.

COVENANT OF COMPASSION

The pastors in our town took turns on Sunday afternoons directing a worship service in the local nursing home. When it was our turn, Fred and I would go. We would sing a few songs, and after a while Fred would give a message. When he was finished we would pray for the people. Not long after our first visit, an elderly lady of about seventy years named Clara approached me. She asked me, "Debby, would you please come, play the piano and teach a Bible lesson for the elderly during the week?" I wasn't sure I wanted to add something else to my busy week, but I knew there was something special about Clara. Her request was so pure and kind. She was not a resident of the home, even though she was older than many of them. She was a volunteer. This was her mission field, and she was passionate

> God sowed His very being into this world in the body of Jesus, so He could reap by Covenant, a people of Covenant.

about her call. Never had I seen someone so devoted. Her prayer life was remarkable, and her commitment irreproachable. Everyone in town knew Clara as a woman of God. I found myself saying yes to her request, but then as my busy week approached, I regretted the commitment. Nevertheless I went. I had grand ideas of how wonderful it was that this older woman had recognized my ministry and wanted me to come. I studied and came prepared with what I thought was a splendid message.

I arrived just as Clara was wheeling a few more elderly people into the activity center. While the wheelchairs were being brought into the room, I began to play the piano. Some of the residents sang with me, but others started making noises; a few even yelled. Someone's urine bag began to leak out onto the floor, and a nurse came running in to clean it up. An old man just stared vacantly at me, while drool ran down his chin.

I thought, "Why am I here? What possible good could I do in this place? I should tell Clara this just won't work for me. I am too busy!" Then I looked at her expectant eyes, and saw a love for these people that only Jesus could have put there. I watched her as she lovingly cared for everyone in the room, even those who were younger then herself. She nodded to me, the clue that it was time to share my message. I stood up and placed my Bible on their lectern. Looking out at the small crowd, I noticed several people's eyes sparkle with desire to hear God's Word. There were others who desperately needed an encouraging hug or prayer. I shared my message proudly, but then I shamefully realized that it had no passion compared to the living message of Clara's life.

When I was ready to leave, Clara asked if I would come again the next week. I heard myself saying yes, and wondered why I did. She also asked if she could call me sometime and pray with me. I said yes to this as well.

This was the beginning of many years of friendship with Clara. She would always encourage me with how well she thought I did sharing my little messages at the nursing home. She taught me more than I ever taught her. She taught me about a Covenant of compassion. She showed me selfless devotion to people who could never repay her kindness. She showed me what it meant to honor the Covenant even when one is tired and old. In a way I had never seen before, Clara showed me the friendship love that Jesus spoke about.

Greater love hath no man than this, that a man lay down his life for his friends. **John 15:13**

The greatest thing Clara showed me was Covenant intercession. Often Clara would call me, and ask, "Do you have a little time for a word of prayer?" I knew that when Clara said, "a little time for a word of prayer", it meant at least an hour. At first I resented this intrusion into my life because it seemed she would call at all the wrong times. Soon, however I found myself calling her, and asking if *she* had "a little time for a word of prayer". I began to treasure the Covenant friendship I had with this woman. I also began to realize that I had imparted little to her; instead, she had been teaching me. Always she would tell me how much she enjoyed our prayer time. She spoke with humility, treating me with the utmost respect. I found Covenant intercession to be a vehicle right to the heart of God. We prayed for our town, the churches, and unsaved family members. The list was endless. We would pray until it seemed we had entered right into the Holy Place.

Clara passed away a few years ago, but I will never forget our Covenant of intercession. She truly was a Covenant maker. She was a **Keeper of Salt**!

THE HEART OF A COVENANT MAKER

Let's look at King David in the Bible. David was a Covenant maker. As I read the account of his life, I am amazed to see how many Covenants he made. However, David did not keep all his Covenants. For example, consider the story of David and Bathsheba. Although many people think that David's greatest sin was his sin with

Bathsheba, the prophet Nathan didn't admonish him for this sin. Instead, Nathan rebuked David for his sin against Uriah. Remember the story?[2] David looked at Bathsheba and desired her. Then, he asked her to come over to his house. After they slept together, Bathsheba found out that she was pregnant. While this was happening, Uriah had been off to war, and David knew that everyone would know that this baby didn't belong to Uriah. In a desperate attempt, David ordered that Uriah be placed in the heat of battle where he would certainly die.

To understand this story, it is important that we understand the relationship that Uriah had with David. Uriah was a foreigner who had sworn allegiance to Israel. Because of Uriah's Covenant with David as his king, he was made a commander in the army. David was likewise obligated to protect and do no harm to Uriah. But David did not honor his Covenant with Uriah. Instead, he stole his wife, then had Uriah killed as a cover up. David broke his Covenant with Uriah twice in a row!

After David's sin against Uriah, the Word of the Lord came to Nathan the prophet. Nathan told David that the sword would never leave his house. In **Malachi 2:16** the prophet Malachi prophesied that one who breaks Covenant, is like one who is covered with violence and puts on a garment of treachery.[3] Treachery is treason, a coup d'état. Treachery is exactly what David did to Uriah. In essence, Nathan was saying to David, "You have broken Covenant with Uriah, and now you are covered with violence, for you have put on a garment of treachery." [4] The result of this broken Covenant was a curse of violence.

Ultimately, David was forgiven for his sin against Uriah. Although David never lost his position as king, he nevertheless, suffered many violent consequences from his broken Covenant. What I find most wonderful is that throughout all this time, David remained a Covenant maker with God. He failed, but he was not a failure. David was by nature a Covenant maker, but like all mankind, he also had a sinful nature. On the other hand, David's predecessor, King Saul was by nature a Covenant breaker. The Bible is full of stories of Saul's broken Covenants. Even the day before Saul died, he broke his Covenant with God by visiting a witch[5]. Both David and Saul broke Covenants, yet David had found the secret.

After Nathan rebuked David with the Word of the Lord, David cried out to God.[6] David knew that he needed to be washed from his sin. He asked God for mercy. David's heart was broken with the possibility that the Lord would cast him away from His presence. He begged God to restore him by renewing his Covenant. David realized that he must humble himself in order to once again become a Covenant maker. It was brokenness, a heart for God and true repentance that distinguished David from Saul. Thus the difference between a Covenant keeper and a Covenant breaker is the difference between a hard heart and a repentant heart.

We have all broken Covenants, but by the mercy of God, we don't have to be Covenant breakers. We can still be Covenant makers. Perhaps you have suffered the pain of a broken Covenant. Maybe you were the one who broke the Covenant. If so, you are at a crossroad, and you can choose to be either like David or like Saul. You can be like Saul by hardening your heart and saying bad things about your former Covenant friend (or spouse).

You can give the devil glory by having a horrible attitude, making sure everyone else around you has a bad attitude too. You can be unrepentant before God, becoming a Covenant breaker, and ultimately suffer the consequences of a violent and bitter life. Or, you can choose to be like David. You can forgive those who wronged you as you ask forgiveness for your own sins. You can be like David and humble yourself.

Covenant makers realize that they are not perfect, that inevitably, sometimes they will break a Covenant. However, they do not let pride keep them from asking for forgiveness and renewing those Covenants. Covenant makers have a heart like David's, whose one fear was that he may be "cast away" from God's presence.

> *We have all broken Covenants, but by the mercy of God, we don't have to be Covenant breakers. We can still be Covenant makers.*

If you have suffered a broken Covenant, by your own fault or not, there is hope. In the midst of pain, God honored David's soft heart and made his Covenant beautiful again. He used Bathsheba to be the mother of the next king of Israel, who would continue the genealogical line to Jesus, the Messiah. Yes, David was a Covenant maker as well as a Covenant Keeper. Yes, *you* can be a Covenant maker. Don't let past failure stop you. Be like David. Be a **Keeper of Salt!**

God has good things for you and your family. They are part of His Covenant with you as His child. When you enter into God's new Covenant, many promises become yours."

— Marilyn Hickey

CHAPTER 7

PROMISES OF COVENANT

SOWERS IN THE KINGDOM OF GOD

One morning the Lord awakened me. He told me that if I would wake up, He would give me a vision of Covenant. It was too early to wake up. Nevertheless, I reluctantly sat up and propped myself with pillows so I wouldn't fall back to sleep. Then I waited. Nothing seemed to happen, but I decided I had nothing to lose by waiting a little longer. Finally I saw something. It was a small seed with a finger pointing toward the inside of the seed. Then I saw the seed in the ground grow into a great big plant. I was expecting something grand, but this small seed didn't seem very grand. It also didn't seem very much like a vision. Then the Lord began to speak to me.

He said, "Inside every seed is the essence of Covenant. The seed has, inside itself, the potential for a multiplied harvest. It is the Promise, or Covenant of Seed Time and Harvest. This is why sowing is so important, and why I want My people to be sowers in the Kingdom of God. This is why it's so important that you learn to be a giver. If you give, your gift will give birth to a multiplied harvest."

Sowing is an example of who God is. He is the Master Giver. He is the Great Sower. In Him are all the promises of Covenant. He told us if we would sow, we would reap a great harvest.[1] He said if we give, more would be given to us.[2] God sowed His very being into this world in the body of Jesus, so He could reap by Covenant, a people of Covenant.[3] What a glorious promise! What a glorious Covenant! Conversely, we must beware lest we become a sower of discontent or criticism, reaping a harvest of discord, stress, bitterness and sickness.

Luke 6:38 says, "Give and it shall be given unto you pressed down and running over". I have noticed that no matter how much I give, I can't give more than what I'm blessed in return. There is a song Bill Gaither wrote that says, "I could never, never out-love the Lord". I think we could easily change the words to "I could never, never out-give the Lord". However, there is more to giving than just expecting a return. When God speaks to us about giving our time, money, or things, He is asking us to *act* like Him. He wants us to experience the wonders of Covenant. It is then that the blessings come.

When I was nineteen, my mom and dad gave me a beautiful white jacket with a white fur-trimmed hood for Christmas. My parents were pastoring a small church at the time, so I knew that the jacket was a real sacrifice for them. I just loved that jacket. I didn't exactly need the jacket since I had a nice winter dress coat, but it was exactly what I wanted. A student in Bible school at the time, I was excited to take that coat with me to school after the Christmas holidays.

When I returned to school, I showed my new jacket to my friends. One of the girls in particular seemed to really like it. In fact, she liked it so much she wanted to borrow it all of the time. I began to notice that sometimes the jacket didn't even make it back to my room between borrowings. Sometimes I didn't see my jacket for a week at a time. I began to talk to some of my other friends about the situation. I asked them, "Why do you think this girl is always borrowing my new jacket? She doesn't return it when she says she will, and I seldom see it anymore."

> *Sowing is an example of who God is. He is the Master Giver. He is the Great Sower. In Him are all the promises of Covenant.*

One of my friends replied, "Well, you see, she doesn't have a winter coat or a winter jacket. It's so cold that some days her lightweight jacket just isn't warm enough. She really means to return it, but the days seem to blur into one another. The next thing she knows, it has been a whole week and she hasn't returned it. I really don't think she means to be unkind. She just doesn't have a coat to keep her warm."

I remembered when John the Baptist said that if you have two coats, give one to your neighbor who has none.[4] I knew the Lord was speaking to me, but I really liked the jacket. It was brand new, so I argued with Him. I hadn't even had much of a chance to wear it. I really didn't feel like giving it away, but one day I found myself telling the girl to just keep the jacket, and not to bother returning it. It was now hers.

I found a beautiful long coat in an expensive department store about three years later. I just loved it! It looked nice and warm, and the style was classic. I was sure that it would be wonderful to wear in the soon coming winter. Whenever I visited the store, I would look at the beautiful coat. One day, I noticed it was on sale! I decided I really needed a new coat, so I purchased it on layaway. I paid a little on my coat each week, and I looked forward in anticipation to the day I could take it home. When I finally paid off the balance, I took my new coat home.

I had been enjoying my new coat for about a month, when one day I found myself counseling a single mother in our church. She had four small children, and seemed to struggle with every situation in her life. There was never enough food to eat or money to pay the bills. Each daughter had a different father, and each father added complication to her discouraging situation. I remember sitting on the floor of the nursery holding her as she cried. Suddenly I noticed her shabby old coat. It was then that I heard the Lord say, "Give her your coat". Well, this order sounded painfully familiar; God had told me to do this once before. Of course I didn't really want to give away my new coat. I hadn't worn it much, and I loved it. But right in my arms was a young mother who needed the coat much more than I did, and I just couldn't say no. I felt like the Lord was saying, "In as much as you have done it unto these, you have done it unto Me."[5] I knew that I would never knowingly turn the Lord away, and I also knew that giving my coat to this young mother was like giving it to the Lord. Jesus wanted this woman to know that He loved her, and that He was watching out for her. He wanted her to know that He cared if she was cold. And he wanted her to know these things through the gift of my coat.

She left the church that day wearing my new coat along with a new smile. I hope she was encouraged. I hope she heard the Lord say, "If I care about you being cold, don't you think I will care for all of the other situations in your life?"

Ever since my two experiences with giving away coats, I always seem to have an abundance of coats. When Fred and I left our church to become missionaries in Russia, I gathered up most of my coats and jackets and just gave them away. After a short time in Russia, we felt called to tropical Africa. I looked at my still large, stack of coats and thought, "I really don't need all of these coats; I might as well give some more away." So I bundled all but a few, and gave them away. This wasn't so hard, since I didn't think I would need any coats in Africa, and I still had so many. I am amazed by the over-abundance of coats that I now have once again. As fast as I give my coats away, the Lord gives me more in abundance.

Fred has had a similar experience with shirts. It seems that no matter how many shirts Fred gives away, he has more than he needs. Last year he commented to me that he had too many shirts, and he wanted to give some away. He did, and within a few weeks he had more shirts than he had before he gave the others away! We began to joke about the "shirt-blessing" because it was so comical.

Each time he would give away one or two, he would get three or four more.

I have found this giving principle to be effective with shoes, dresses, time, money, furniture and food. No matter what I give, the Lord blesses me, giving me more in return. It's fun to watch to see what the Lord will do.

The principle of "sowing and reaping" is a key element of Covenant. When we sow in Covenant relationship with our Lord, He is bound by Covenant to multiply it to us, and give to us a "blessing we cannot contain." The same is true in our earthly Covenants. Whatever we sow into the life of another person, we reap. If we sow love, we reap love. If we sow friendship, we reap friendship.

Give, and it shall be given unto you; good measure, pressed down, and shaken together, and running over, shall men give into your bosom. For with the same measure that ye mete withal it shall be measured to you again. **Luke 6:38**

I found it interesting that as I sowed coats, I reaped coats. When Fred sowed shirts he reaped shirts. If I sow cake or cookies, I reap cake or cookies. I never have a lack of the things I sow. A farmer sows a specific crop and reaps a specific harvest. Fred and I have not finished sowing, and our harvest is not finished either. There is a Covenant of harvest still to come, because we have been sowing seed.

Now, we should note that sometimes God takes our seed and turns it into something that money and things can't replace. I often think about the times when I, or those I love, could have been killed in car accidents, but were not. I think about the billions of germs waiting to enter my body, but do not. I think about relationships that could have been broken, and they never were. As I lay in bed at night, I often thank the Lord for His faithfulness to me throughout the day and I thank Him that His mercies are new every morning.[6] These are things that money, coats and shirts can't buy, but in the garden of God, they can be produced using any seed God wishes to use. This is so wonderful. With God all things are possible![7]

> ...If thou shalt hearken diligently unto the voice of the LORD thy God, to observe *and* to do all his commandments ... And all these blessings shall come on thee, **AND OVERTAKE THEE** ... Blessed *shalt* thou *be* in the city, and blessed *shalt* thou *be* in the field. Blessed *shall be* the fruit of thy body, and the fruit of thy ground, and the fruit of thy cattle, the increase of thy kine, and the flocks of thy sheep. Blessed *shall be* thy basket and thy store. Blessed *shalt* thou *be* when thou comest in, and blessed *shalt* thou *be* when thou goest out. ... And the LORD shall make thee plenteous in goods, in the fruit of thy body, and in the fruit of thy cattle, and in the fruit of thy ground, in the land ... And the LORD shall make thee the head, and not the tail ... if that thou hearken unto the commandments of the LORD thy God, which I command thee this day, to observe and to do *them*. (Emphasis added) **Deuteronomy 28:1-13**

This passage shows us the many blessings the Children of Israel were offered if they would walk in Covenant. These blessings can be ours as well. The passage even says that these blessings can "overtake" us! So often we run after blessings, but the blessings are really running after us. Instead of fearing the future, wondering how all your needs will be met, remember your blessings are chasing you!

All Covenants have terms, like contracts. Likewise, in order to receive the blessings of Covenant, what does the Lord require of us? **Deuteronomy 28** teaches us that we receive the blessings of Covenant when we follow the commandments of the Lord. How could one possibly follow all of the commands that are listed in the writings of Moses? Wouldn't that be impossible?

For this commandment which I command thee this day, it *is* not hidden from thee, neither *is* it far off. It *is* not in heaven, that thou shouldest say, who shall go up for us to heaven, and bring it unto us, that we may hear it, and do it? Neither *is* it beyond the sea, that thou shouldest say, Who shall go over the sea for us, and bring it unto us, that we may hear it, and do it? But the word *is* very nigh unto thee, in thy mouth, and in thy heart, that thou mayest do it. See, I have set before thee this day life and good, and death and evil; In that I command thee this day to love the LORD thy God, to walk in his ways, and to keep his commandments and his statutes and his judgments, that thou mayest live and multiply: and the LORD thy God shall bless thee in the land whither thou goest to possess it. **Deuteronomy 30:11-16**

If this is so simple, what then is our obligation as New Testament followers of Christ? We surely can't remember all that Moses said, and we surely can't follow all the commands given to the Israelites. So how can we fulfill these obligations and receive the blessings?

Jesus said that He hadn't come to earth to destroy

the Old Law, but to fulfill it.[8] Further, He taught us that
the greatest Law was that we should "love the Lord God
with all of our heart, soul, mind and strength" and the second greatest is that we should "love our neighbor as much
as we love ourselves."[9] Paul said in **Romans 13:8** that
"love" satisfies all the commandments and the requirements of the law. We fulfill the law and all its requirements when we simply choose to walk in a Covenant of
love.[10]

Covenant love is the single most fundamental principle of the Bible. Why did the Lord bless me with an
abundance of coats? It was love; love for God and love
for my neighbor. It is this Covenant that compels us to
sow time in God's presence. It teaches us to hear His
voice, and trains our ears
to forsake all others. This
love propels us to sow into
others' lives and to be a
blessing to them. Cove-
nant love of God is the
most difficult, yet the sim-
plest thing we can do.
Covenant love with God obligates our love for others.
You can give a coat, give a little time, give a prayer, give
some love. This is Covenant with God, this is being a
Keeper of Salt, and this is when we will receive the
blessings of Covenant.

> *We fulfill the law and all
> its requirements when we
> simply choose to walk in a
> Covenant of love.*

Won't you join me? Together we can walk in
Covenant and reap a great harvest. The Covenant is not
too hard to fulfill. Be a blessing, and you will reap a
bountiful harvest. You will be blessed when you become
a **Keeper of Salt!**

He giveth more grace when the burdens grow greater,

He sendeth more strength when the labors increase;

To added affliction he addeth his mercy,

To multiplied trials, His multiplied peace.

— Annie Johnson Flint

CHAPTER 8

COVENANT GRACE

Have you ever compared the lives of Samson and Samuel? I have. The two "Sams" had similar beginnings. Both were born of previously barren women and were destined to lead Israel. Both were dedicated to the Lord in the Nazarite fashion.[1] Both had the Spirit of God come upon them. Both had great gifts. Both led Israel. But only one kept the Covenant.

Before Samson was born, his mother was instructed to raise him as a Nazarite.[2] In Bible times, a Nazarite was a very special person who was in Covenant with God.[3] This Covenant was for a man or woman who made a vow to be separated unto the Lord. He would not eat or drink anything from the grape, he would never cut his hair, and he would be holy. He was never to touch a dead body, even if it was his mother or father. He was to remain separated unto the Lord. In return for this Covenant, the Lord promised Samson's parents that He would use Samson to deliver Israel out of the hands of the Philistines. Samson somehow found himself in the arms of a prostitute, surrounded by Philistines, his hair cut off and the Spirit of the Lord having left him!

Samuel, on the other hand, walked with God, maintained a powerful anointing, and was mourned by all of Israel when he died. He happened to Samson? Why did Samuel succeed and Samson fail? Did Samson fail just because he allowed his hair to be cut, or is there a deeper problem in his life that eroded his foundation long before the haircutting event?

I often contrast the two "Sams" because I don't want to wake up some day and find that the Lord has left me. Like Samson, I don't want to assume that the Lord is with me when He is actually gone. Sometimes I wonder why Samson didn't know the Lord was gone. Didn't he know the presence of the Lord or did he just assume that he was exempt from the requirements of the Lord? How could this happen to one so strong, so anointed, so obviously placed in position by the Lord?

A COVENANT "SET APART"

The Nazarite Covenant is a symbolic picture today of what it is like for those who wish to be separated unto the Lord. Followers of Christ are supposed to be different, and people should notice that. Nazarites looked and acted differently. Similarly, as followers of Christ, we should be separated from the rest of the world.[4] There is a phrase in an old poem that says, "Others may, but you may not." Samson understood this well. He was called to live by a different standard; it was part of his Covenant. Likewise, the Covenant you have with God may require you to live your life differently than those around you. You may even think some of the requirements are silly, but if it is part of your Covenant, you must follow these requirements or you may miss out on the presence of the Lord. Even worse, He may not be there when you need Him.

This principle of being "set apart" can be understood in this story: Years ago my brother Thom went on a trip to Haiti. He was with a whole group of young people who were doing some building and ministry. In the middle of the trip the group leader decided that they should have a day of sightseeing. So everyone went off for a nice day of the sights. Coming upon a Voodoo temple, the director decided it would be interesting for the young people to see inside. My brother instantly felt in his heart that this would be a bad thing for him to do, and so he refused to go into the temple. Scoffing at his refusal the group smugly entered, leaving Thom behind. Thom might have felt foolish standing outside the temple, alone, but he certainty didn't feel foolish when later that day he was the only one in the group who didn't get dysentery. Thom kept Covenant with the leading of the Holy Spirit in his heart. He was a **Keeper of Salt**!

1 Peter 2:9 tells us that we are a chosen generation, a royal priesthood and a holy nation. We are God's special, Covenant people. We were taken out of darkness, for **Ephesians 5:11** tells us we have no fellowship with the darkness any more. I have had many opportunities to enter places of voodoo and witchcraft in Africa, but I have no desire to enter. Many times I have refused to even enter the shop of an artisan because of the numerous occult items on display. Once you have entered into a Covenant with God, and your life is now His, you are much the same as a Nazarite, dedicated to Him. Because you are in Covenant, what others may do you may not!

NO RESPECT FOR COVENANT

Samson was called to keep the special Covenant requirements of a Nazarite. The Nazarite's hair was a symbol of this Covenant; cutting the hair was a symbol of the end of it.[5] When a Nazarite was finished with his vows, he would cut his hair and give an offering to the Lord. He was then released from his vow.

Early in Samson's life, he looked at the Philistine women and desired one for his wife. His parents begged him to find a nice girl among the Israelites, but Samson determined to follow his own desires, choosing a wife from the enemy, something that was strictly forbidden under his Covenant.[6] Maybe Samson's parents didn't teach him to value the Covenant, or maybe he thought it simply didn't apply to him. Either way, Samson was more interested in satisfying his lusts than in keeping Covenant with God. Instead of looking to God to make him happy, he looked to the enemy. Even worse, he made a Covenant with the enemy by marrying the Philistine woman. Nevertheless, God used this situation to deliver the Israelites from their enemy for a number of years, as Samson judged them. As in the story of Joseph when his brothers sold him into slavery, what was intended for evil, God used for good.[7] However, Samson reaped nothing but pain from his sin. He lost the item of his affection (the girl) and he still was not happy.

Samson violated his Covenant again by touching dead animals. According to the Nazarite Covenant,

Nazarites were never allowed to touch a dead body. However, on two occasions Samson touched a dead lion.[8] Then he touched the bone of a freshly killed donkey.[9] Not only did Samson touch these dead bodies, but in the case of the dead lion, he ate honey from a honeycomb inside the carcass and gave the honey to his parents.

Samson's whole life seemed to be one of disrespect for the Covenant. He slept with prostitutes and even gave his heart to one named Delilah. Three times Delilah begged Samson to tell her the secret of his strength; each time Samson told her a story that was not true. She believed what Samson said and told his enemy, the Philistines. Of course they trapped him, but Samson was so strong each time he was able to become free. Delilah began to feel like a fool. Samson was spending a lot of time in the arms of Delilah, and he obviously wanted to make her happy. He really desired to please her, so he humored her by giving her false reasons for his strength. I've often wondered why Samson didn't realize that Delilah was trapping him. Each time he fell asleep, the things he told her were done to him. Did he think that the Covenant was just a game, or was he trapped in something even more deadly? The Bible doesn't say, but I wonder if Samson had begun to break another Nazarite Covenant by drinking wine. How else could he have his hair woven into a cloth and tightened into a loom without being awakened? Maybe he was addicted to alcohol and to the thrill of doing forbidden things. This could be the reason he was willing to confide in Delilah time and time again, even after he was betrayed. If this is true, then we see yet another area in which Samson didn't respect his Covenant. Finally Samson told Delilah the truth. He explained the Nazarite Covenant and the vow to never cut his hair. Knowing Delilah would betray him once again just like the three times before, Samson betrayed the Covenant.

"And she said, The Philistines be upon thee, Samson. And he awoke out of his sleep, and said, I will go out as at other times before, and shake myself. And he wist not that the LORD was departed from him." **Judges 16:20**

When Samson's hair was cut, he was released from his vow, for his Nazarite Covenant was finished. Once the Lord left Samson, he lost his strength. The Philistines finally had Samson right where they wanted him. They gouged out his eyes and forced him to live as a slave.

Although, Samson had a lot of power, he had no respect for the Covenant. Sadly, this is what happens with many people today. Samson had a great gift, but he seemed to glory in the gift instead of the presence of the Lord. Samuel was gifted too, yet his pleasure was in the presence of the Lord. Therefore, Samuel walked in an unusual grace, Covenant Grace. Samson didn't walk in the Covenant; he walked in the power of his gifts. As a result, he forfeited the grace of the Covenant.

I wonder what it must have been like for Samuel on the day he was left with Eli the priest. Imagine what it must have been like for a small boy to be left alone with a strange old man, yet Samuel never became bitter. He wasn't angry with God for the Covenant his mother had made. He didn't ever seem to resent the direction which his life took.[10]

Samson, in comparison, lived a life of anger. As a result, there was no grace in his life. Many forfeit the grace that could be theirs for the momentary satisfaction of bitterness and anger. Our excuses for bitterness and anger often seem justified by the inequality of our lives. There are people in ministry, including spouses and their children, who forfeit grace because they resent the cost of their Covenant. How sad it is for me to see so many pastors' children run from God because of bitterness and unforgiveness. Like Samuel, whose mother chose his Covenant for him, there is a special grace for those who choose to walk in Covenant, even the Covenant of their parents. Personally, I watch the Lord bless my children as they honor the Covenants I have made. They walk under an unusual grace.

> *Many forfeit the grace that could be theirs for the momentary satisfaction of bitterness and anger.*

There is a cost, too, for all those in Covenant. For example Hannah gave up her first son for Covenant. Samuel gave up a normal childhood, and instead chose to keep his mother's Covenant by living with a strange old priest in the temple. Many lives were positively and eternally affected as the result of these kept Covenants. While Hannah's kept Covenant changed a nation, Samson's broken Covenant destroyed his life, as he died alone with his enemy.

COVENANTS OF SLAVERY VS. COVENANTS OF FREEDOM

These are the two covenants; the one from the mount Sinai, which gendereth to bondage... But Jerusalem which is above is free, which is the mother of us all. Nevertheless what saith the scripture? Cast out the bondwoman and her son: for the son of the bondwoman shall not be heir with the son of the freewoman. So then, brethren, we

are not children of the bondwoman, but of the free.
Galatians 4:24-31

The Apostle Paul explains two kinds of Covenants in **Galatians 4:24**, the Covenant of slavery and the Covenant of freedom. We have all been under the Covenant of slavery before we became followers of Christ. We were bound in sin, in Covenant with the devil - and he tried to consume us. There are many bad Covenants of slavery in our world today, like the Covenant a drug dealer has with his suppliers and the Covenant a prostitute has with her evil employer. Not a drug dealer or a prostitute? Maybe you can relate to the Covenant of slavery which so many people have with gambling, overeating or any other compulsive and self-destructive behavior. Bad Covenants can suck the life out of us and destroy us. The problem is that even bad Covenants, when broken, can leave scars.

In 1987 I had cancer. Like a Covenant of slavery, it was trying to consume me, and had to be cut out or it would have killed me. When I discovered the cancer, I went to a surgeon who cut me open, and cut out the cancer. In doing this, he also took more than the cancer to make sure he had all of the disease. There was a separation of the good parts of my body as well as the bad. Because the surgery was traumatic and it took me months to feel like myself again. The scars I have on my body from the surgery will probably be with me for the rest of my life. They are a memorial to something that wanted to kill me but is no longer a part of my life. I experienced a violent separation with cancer, but it was something I had to endure in order to live. When we are involved in a bad Covenant, it's like a cancer to us. It wants to kill us.

When Samson lost his eyesight, it was a physical

example of how blind he had become in his spirit. He was a fool. He had made a Covenant with his enemy, which had become a part of him, thus making it difficult for him to break free. Samson's bad Covenant became a bloody Covenant mess, eventually costing him his life.

Bad Covenants are the plan of the devil. The only way to escape is to come to Jesus the Master Surgeon. He will cut out the bad Covenant and make a new one. The Good News is that God makes all things new.[11] He can take that which has been death to us, cut it out, and make us new. The promised New Covenant is the Covenant of freedom that sets us free from sin and death. Therefore we don't have to live in the bondage of slavery.

EMBRACE THE GRACE

We all live under Covenants. We have Covenants with our spouse, our children, our employer, our pastor, our friends, even with our bank. Perhaps, like Samson and Samuel, you had no choice in the Covenant. Do you respect these Covenants? Do you honor the Spirit of Grace?

We have all heard stories of pastor's children who walk away from the Lord. I have seen spouses grow bitter because of Covenants their mate has made to Christian ministry. I have seen similar situations with the spouses and children of those in the military and other public services. In all these examples these people didn't choose the Covenant; it was made for them. My heart breaks when I think about what people have missed because they refused to honor these Covenants.

> For the mountains shall depart, and the hills be removed; but my kindness shall not depart from thee, neither shall the covenant of my peace be removed, saith the LORD that hath mercy on thee.
> **Isaiah 54:10**

Wonderful grace and peace can be ours when we reconcile with our Covenant, even those which we didn't choose. Even though our lives are full of situations that are beyond our control, the Covenant contains grace beyond measure, and blessings that cannot be counted. In the Covenant an anointing exists that far surpasses even what others may have. Samuel was the greatest judge Israel ever had, yet he wasn't the one who made the Covenant, his mother did. All he did was honor the Covenant and walk in the grace that was his.

If you have broken Covenants, or if you have made bad Covenants, don't give up. God is not finished with you. Realize that these Covenants are a wonderful opportunity for God to change your situation and shower you with

> *There is wonderful grace and peace that is ours when we reconcile with our Covenant, even those which we didn't choose.*

His grace. So choose to embrace the grace. Be at peace with your Covenants. Make the Covenants others have made for you, your own. In doing so, you will be surprised by the supernatural grace and peace in your life. Be a **Keeper of Salt**!

NOTES:

False friends are like a shadow, keeping close to us while we walk in the sunshine, but leaving us when we cross into the shade.

— Christian Bovee

Rejection is the sand in the oyster; the irritant that ultimately produces the pearl.

— Burke Wilkinson

CHAPTER 9

MADNESS

There is probably no better example of an unreciprocated Covenant, than the story of King Saul. Saul had unreciprocated Covenants with both God and his successor, David. Sadly though, Saul was unfaithful to his Covenants and therefore, lost his blessings. Four times in **Deuteronomy 28** we see that if we break our Covenants, we come under the curse of mental and emotional stress. [1] As a result of Saul's broken Covenants, he lost his mind, his place on the throne, and many of his children. Furthermore, Saul himself died an untimely death. [2]

Before David became king, David and Saul knew each other well, for they were in Covenant. David offered his services to King Saul. After Saul's broken Covenant with God, David played music to soothe the king. Then David fought the giant Goliath who was a great enemy of Israel. David's victory was rewarded with the hand of Saul's daughter in marriage. Thus David was bound, not only in a patriotic Covenant with King Saul, but also as the king's son-in-law. David felt such a connection to Saul that he called him, "father." [3] They ate at the same table and shared the same food. Having become a part of Saul's family, and he expected to receive the blessings of this Covenant relationship.

Imagine David's shock and surprise when Saul, in his jealousy and madness, began to throw spears at him! Amazingly, David stayed, dodging the spears for quite some time until eventually he had no choice but to leave. Yet David never fought back, and he never threw a spear. In trying to kill David, Saul chased him all over the mountains and forced him into hiding. He even gave David's wife to another man! Yet David lived a life of Covenant and practiced "love enduring all things" long before the Apostle Paul wrote these words. [4] Covenant was a part of David's being.

David lived through the heartrending experience of an unreciprocated Covenant, guarding the life of his beloved king Saul, even when others begged him to kill him. [5] David was a Covenant keeper, who would keep his side of the Covenant even if Saul did not. Saul called David his enemy while David called Saul his father. He loved Saul, and the unreciprocated Covenant must have broken his heart.

THE ONLY EXPLANATION, MADNESS

Not only did David suffer an unreciprocated Covenant with Saul, but experienced the same pain later with his own son, when Absalom turned against his father and tried to take the kingdom from him. [6] What a heartbreak this must have been for David. He must have wondered if

God had forsaken him. Yet he never fought his son, but freely left the kingdom in the Lord's hands. He had no desire to break his Covenant with his son, even though Absalom did not keep Covenant with him. In the end, God honored David, and the kingdom was restored, although it cost Absalom his life. We should note that David would have rather lost the kingdom than for his son to die. [7]

I have a friend who, for years felt he was in Covenant with a certain group of people. Some of them had walked together for as many as twenty years. They worked together as fathers and brothers, who loved each other, prayed for each other, and sacrificed for each other. After some disagreements, however, our friend was dismissed from the group. Not only was he dismissed, but he was also considered "unforgivable", and others were told to avoid him. After several attempts on his part to reconcile, he began to realize that he was in an unreciprocated Covenant. He told us that the saddest part of this chapter in his life was that he loved and trusted these men. He felt they were fathers and brothers to him. Our friend thought that according to Covenant, if he were in error, then the others would seek him out and help him to stay true to God. But once the others felt our friend was in error, they disclaimed him, threw him out, and never tried to rescue him.

If this isn't madness, I don't know what is. Even in the business world people are given a chance to make things right. Too often in the church we write people off, never giving them another chance. One of the wonderful things about my friend is that he looks longingly at the past situation, wishing that the relationships had never been broken, and never saying anything bad about the people who hurt him. He's a **Keeper of Salt.**

Fred and I have had several unreciprocated Covenants. Years ago, for example, we did some Christian work with a new organization. We dearly loved the people in the organization and felt a strong tie, which we thought was Covenant. Several times we expressed our commitment to the director and thought the Covenant had been reciprocated. It wasn't. Soon the director began to cool off towards us; eventually communication stopped. It was heart breaking. We tried several times to contact him, but he would not return our calls or respond to e-mails. We spoke to several mutual friends, and checked our phone numbers and e-mail address just in case we had the wrong information. It has been several years since then, yet we still consider this man to be our friend. We have wonderful memories of our relationship. He imparted a lot into our ministry. It is sad indeed that he is lost to us. How wonderful it would be if he realized how much Fred and I still love him, and still desire his friendship.

DON'T THROW SPEARS

The Lord often reminds me of the story of David's unreciprocated Covenant with Saul. The Lord also reminds me that, just like David, I mustn't retaliate. Perhaps these hurtful people are in my life for a reason. If God is trying to speak to me through these people, then I must be careful to listen to what they have to say. Just think, *I* could be the one who is wrong in this situation! Even David considered the possibility that he might be wrong.[8] That's why he was careful to not harm or make any accusation against Saul, or even against his own son Absalom. Although there have been times when I have found myself throwing spears of criticism against those who have hurt me, I thank the Lord who still works out all things for my good and helps me when I am weak. It's my desire that I would never be skilled in the art of spear throwing. I wouldn't want to wound the one whom I should love as my own. Perhaps if I am careful to not throw any spears of revenge, or anything barbed with hurt and bitterness, these lost Covenant friends will return to me. With God, all things are possible!

> *Keep your side of the Covenant even when others don't. Remember, God is interested in your heart. God doesn't excuse us from unreciprocated Covenants. He looks to see what the response of our heart will be.*

God honored King David for his faithfulness to the Covenant with Saul and Absalom, even though it was un-reciprocated. Because David was a true **Keeper of Salt,** God blessed him accordingly. My friend (earlier in this chapter), who was rejected by his fathers and brothers in the Lord, also says that God has greatly used the unreciprocated situation in his life to do many wonderful things in him. God has blessed him with many true Covenant relationships since then. In my own life I have seen some of my one-way Covenants become two-way. For those that remain one-way, I still have hope. I know that God will bless me if I am true to my side of the Covenant.

It would be a wonderful world indeed if we could live in the peace and security which comes from Covenant. I wish we could all be *one* as Jesus prayed. [9] I wish the strife, backbiting and gossip would cease. I wish there was peace on earth and goodwill to men. Without Covenant, however, these things will never be ours. If Christians kept their Covenants, there would be no more church splits and or divisions. The world would see Christ's Body as a glorious Bride, without spot or wrinkle. Even more remarkable, they would be jealous. The world would long for our Bridegroom. We would become the envy of all the other religions. It's the power, the peace, and the love that belongs to those who live in true covenant with their Creator and with their brothers that people of other religions desire.

> *If Christians kept their Covenants, there would be no more church splits and or divisions. The world would see Christ's Body as a glorious Bride, without spot or wrinkle, and even more remarkable, they would be jealous.*

Be a Covenant keeper. Keep your side of the Covenant even when others don't. Remember, God is interested in *your* heart. God doesn't excuse us from unreciprocated Covenants. He looks to see what the response of our heart will be. Yes, it hurts to make Covenants with someone and then have that person reject us, but God is looking for a Covenant people who will look beyond the hurt. Be a **Keeper of Salt**!

NOTES:

The Holy Ghost alone is in the true position of a critic; he is able to show what is wrong without wounding and hurting.

— Oswald Chambers

When we persecute and hurt the children of God, we are but persecuting God and hurting ourselves far more.

— A. B. Simpson

CHAPTER 10

SPILLERS OF THE SALT

The telephone rang, and the pastor on the other line said, "You have to choose, you know. People expect you to take sides."

Take sides? What on earth could that be all about? The person went on to tell me about the recent quarreling going on in our fellowship. As a result of many disagreements in the leadership, the battle lines had been drawn. People were expected to take sides. To take sides would mean leaving behind friends, for we had many on both sides. The idea was unthinkable.

I remember responding in shock, saying, "But we don't want to take sides." The response was, "If you don't, your side will be chosen for you."

Fred and I tried to walk the fine line of both sides. It wasn't easy. The problem was that once we chose to maintain friendship with one side, the other side saw us as the enemy. It was a heartbreaking situation.

I may never figure out exactly why this all happened, but the bottom line was that there was a quarrel and a lot of unforgiveness. Eventually, the fellowship fell apart and the people were scattered. In the process friends were separated from friends. Many hearts were broken, and I fear that some have never been mended. The cause? I don't know; just some quarrel that I never did really understand. It's hard to even remember what some of those issues were today. In the light of eternity, I wonder if the quarrel was really worth it. I don't think so. Taking sides in the church doesn't make sense to me. After all, aren't we all followers of Christ? Aren't we supposed to be on the *same* side?

CHILDISH FIGHTING

In **Acts 15:36-41**, we read of Paul and Barnabas. They had been a great and anointed team, yet they had heated argument which escalated to the point that their friendship was broken.[1] Although God turned this situation around for good, and the Gospel was preached in twice as many places as before, their Covenant friendship still suffered a horrible separation. Their salt had been spilled.

The phrase s*pilling of salt*, comes from two people threatening to quarrel as though they had already broken friendship.[2] As I travel the world I have seen churches quarreling, with broken friendships multiplying, until there is little trust between anyone. The stories are the same, only the names change. As Solomon says in **Eccle-**

siastes 1:9, there is surely nothing new under the sun. Hurting pastors and congregations fill our churches. No wonder the world thinks the church has little to offer them.

Colossians 3:13 says we should forgive one another. Forgiveness is so wonderful because it is more than just forgetting the offense; it's choosing not to fight about it. It's choosing to walk in peace and find some way to stay in Covenant. We are to be gentle with our brothers and sisters, not saying unkind things or picking fights over issues that really aren't important.

I heard of one church where the pastor and the assistant pastor had a fistfight in the front yard. I know of another where the pastor and his father didn't speak for years. One, a church almost split over the color of the carpet! It would be funny if it wasn't true! I remember one couple telling me that, since they were now Christians, they wouldn't visit their "un-saved" family for Christmas. In effect, they used their salvation as an excuse for a broken relationship. Situations like these happen everyday. Churches split, friendships split and families split. Everyday people quarrel, and pay a great price for their right to fight.

The Bible talks about vain arguing.[3] I am sure that most people feel they have a just cause to fight. They would probably even argue their right to argue. You probably know some people like this. Fighters are difficult people to be with. They always have an issue that they are upset about, and they are always ready to fight. When I can, I avoid these people because it costs me too much. A wise man counts the cost before he goes into battle. Even if I know that I am "right" in an argument, the cost of hurting, or even losing my friend is too great. I have quarreled and won, only to find out that it is very lonely in the middle of the winner's circle. The anticipated pleasure of victory seems pale in light of the lost blessings. I don't always have to be right, but I do have to always keep my Covenants.

I have never been a fan of cruel teasing. I am afraid it's just spilling salt. It's not building one another up; it's tearing each other down. One day while some men were working on our church building, I heard one of the men comment on

> *I don't always have to be right, but I do have to always keep my Covenants.*

how fat one of the other workers was. I saw a fleeting look of sorrow on the heavier man's face. Quickly he recovered and threw a teasing comment right back. A few weeks later, I overheard the same men talking. The same "fat" comments started to fly around the room. Most people thought this was all funny and just a game, but as I watched, I saw looks of hurt and sadness in the eyes of some of the men. It wasn't long before their friendships started to deteriorate. It wasn't fun and games. It was spilling salt, once you spill salt, it is hard to pick it all up again.

How can we be a strong Church if we are tearing each other down? The men working on our church certainly weren't modeling the ideals of Covenant love. **I Corinthians 13** tells us that true love is kind; it doesn't delight in hurting someone else. It always protects and trusts. Love doesn't look for a way to quarrel, but looks for a way to prefer others and humble ourselves. These men should have been looking for ways to honor each other. They thought they were working on our church; the reality was they were tearing it apart.

COVENANT ACCOUNTING

Malachi 3:16-17 tells us what God does with our words. When those who trust in the Lord speak to their friends about God, about His Covenant love, and about His promises, then God writes all these things down in His book.[4] Then when times of trouble come, God gets out His book and remembers what was said. He then rescues those who spoke good things about Him, because they are His treasured possession.

This is exactly what happened to Mordecai the Jew, in the Book of Esther. Mordecai heard about an assassination attempt on the life of King Xerxes. He sent word to Queen Esther that people were plotting to kill the king. She told the king and gave the credit to Mordecai. The assassination attempt was stopped, and the whole record was written down in the history books of the king. But there was no reward given to Mordecai.

Years later, the king couldn't sleep. He asked for someone to open the royal history books and read to him. They read the story of Mordecai saving the king's life. He asked if anything had ever been done for Mordecai to reward him for his faithfulness to the king. The answer was, "No". Later that morning the king's wicked advisor, Haman, came to the palace. The king asked him what should be done for someone that the king desired to honor. Proud Haman, thinking that surely the king would only want to honor him, suggested an elaborate honor that involved dressing the man like the king and parading him before all of the people as if he were a king. King Xerxes thought this was a great idea and told Haman to go do this at once for Mordecai.

The king's remembrance of Mordecai's good deed could not have come at a better time. Haman had been devising a plan to kill all of the Jews for the very reason that Mordecai wouldn't bow down and worship him. Of course, Haman's plan greatly distressed Mordecai and all of the Jews of the land. However, God had saved the record in the king's book for this day of trouble. Mordecai had honored his Covenant with the kin; as a result, Mordecai was honored and his life was saved. Ultimately, God used Mordecai's niece, Ether, to save all of the Jews.

Again Malachi tells us that God keeps a record of both the good things and the bad things we say. If we never have good things to say, then there is nothing good for God to read about in His book. But, if we do have good things to say, we are honoring our Covenant with Him and with others. Then when our day of trouble comes, God gets out His Book and looks to see what we have been saying. When He sees the record, He looks for a way to reward us for our faithfulness to the Covenant, and rescues us from trouble. In fact, it says in **Matthew 12:36**, that we will be held "accountable" for every idle word we say.

God is a Covenant accountant. He keeps a "bank account" for each one of us, from which we can draw when we have trouble. This is why spilling salt is so dangerous. When we argue, criticize or even tease in unkind ways, we are dishonoring our Covenant to God and to our friends, rather than making "deposits" into our account. When our day of trouble comes, we may have nothing to draw from.

How full is your Covenant account? Have your spilled Covenants left you vulnerable in your day of trouble? Has always being "right" left you disappointed?

> God is a Covenant accountant. He keeps a "bank account" for each one of us, from which we can draw when we have trouble.

Maybe you've spilled your salt, and lost a few friends and family members along the way. Maybe the emptiness you feel is because you really are empty. Maybe you've lost blessings, peace, and loved ones because your Covenant account is overdrawn. I want to keep my Covenants with God, my family, and my friends. I want my Covenant account to be full. Join me. Together we will be **Keepers of Salt**.

God is so good that he only awaits our desire to overwhelm us with the gift of himself.

— François Fénelon

CHAPTER 11

ONE-SIDED COVENANTS

I met up with an old friend of mine during a recent conference. She told me about her daughter and some on-going situations she was facing. I made a commitment to pray for this girl, a commitment I intended to keep. This was a one-sided Covenant; I have a Covenant with her, although she does not have Covenant with me. I don't expect anything from her, and she is still completely unaware of my commitment to her.

God makes one-sided Covenants as well. He made a Covenant with us that there would be day and night. There are no requirements on our part for Him to fulfill His promise. He made the seasons. Still, He expects nothing from us. He promised to never again destroy the earth by flood, yet again, we have no obligation whatso-ever. Jesus died for our sins in a Covenant of salvation, promising to return to earth again some day. Nothing I do will ever change those facts.

Although God never breaks His one-sided Covenants, unfortunately, we often do. In a one-sided Covenant, generally the other party is not aware of the commitment that has been made. As a result, one-sided Covenants often lack accountability. Sometimes only God knows if the promise is kept.

I once asked a woman to pray for me on a regular basis. She said, no! Offended, I asked her, why? She told me that the Lord had not directed her to pray for me, and that she had many people she prayed for already. What a wise woman! She refused to make a Covenant with me because she knew that she would not be able to keep it. She resisted the people-pleasing temptation to just say "yes" and make me happy. She was a **Keeper of Salt**.

ONE-SIDED COVENANTS OFTEN LEAD TO TWO-SIDED COVENANTS

God's love for us is a one-sided Covenant. If an individual curses God and lives his life for Satan, he or she is still loved by God. Christ's death made another one-sided Covenant to us. His blood gave to us the availability of salvation, which is unconditionally offered to all. Note, salvation is *available* to all, but not *received* by all. To receive salvation, it must be transformed into a two-sided Covenant. We must acknowledge our sin and put our faith in Christ to receive salvation. When we do this, we are making a Covenant back to God. Therefore, salvation is a one-sided Covenant which can lead to a two-sided Covenant.

Proverbs 18:24 A man that hath friends must shew himself friendly.

I have a special Covenant relationship with a woman named Becky. We have a two-sided Covenant, although it wasn't always that way. I met Becky several years ago at the close of a pastor's conference. She walked up to me, and told me that the Lord had instructed her to pray for me. She wasn't just going to pray a short little prayer, but she was going to pray for me all year. Her words were emphatic, and I truly believed that the motive of her heart was sincere. However, I was reminded of how many times I had also said that I would pray for someone and then forgot.

I met up with Becky again at the next year's pastor's conference. I had totally forgotten her commitment to pray for me. To my surprise, she reminded me of her commitment and told me that she had prayed for me all year. My heart was touched. She had made a one-sided Covenant with me, and she had kept it.

> *Wouldn't it be wonderful if we offered one-sided Covenants and, like God, expected nothing in return except the joy of keeping our word?*

When I saw the character of God in her life, I wanted her as my friend. Today we enjoy a special two-sided Covenant friendship, because we pray for *each other*. If she hadn't made her initial one-sided Covenant with me, we might never have become the close friends we are today.

PASSION

While two-sided Covenants often involve little more than mutual agreement, one-sided Covenants require the power of passion. In the thick of humiliation and rejection, it was passion that led Christ to the cross. It was Becky's passion to pray that caused her to commit to intercede for me. It is passion that drives lovers towards each other, neither knowing how the other will respond. Passion gives one-sided Covenant holders the strength to endure loneliness, driving them forward, without thought of reward or returned commitment.

When I was in the hospital recovering from my cancer surgery, a local pastor named Andy came to visit me every day. I had met him once or twice many years before, but I really didn't know him well. Andy wasn't on the hospital chaplain's staff, I had never been a member of his church, and the hospital was not on his way home. Yet, everyday he prayed for me and encouraged me. He didn't have any prophetic words or anything remarkable to say. It was the *fact that he came*, that was remarkable. He showed me a one-sided Covenant of friendship, requiring nothing from me in return. I'll never forget his kindness or the lesson in commitment he taught me. Every day before he left my hospital room we would say, "I'll see you tomorrow". It would have been so easy for him to miss a day. But Andy was a **Keeper of Salt;** I saw him everyday until I returned home.

Most wedding vows include the phrase, "I pledge you my faith". It amazes me that many couples have no idea what they are pledging. Pledging *faith* is a commitment to be *faithful*. Faithfulness *is not* a two-sided Covenant. Rather, it is a commitment to remain faithful even if the other party is not. "I pledge you my faith" contains no words of recompense. Divorce is often the result of a couple who errantly thought their commitment was a two-way street; I'll do for you if you do for me. Those in a healthy marriage realize that their commitment is a one-way street; I'll do for you, regardless of what you do for me.

Wouldn't it be wonderful if we could know for a fact that people would keep their word? Wouldn't it amaze the world if we, as followers of Christ, kept our word even when it cost us our time, money and effort? Wouldn't it be wonderful if we offered one-sided Covenants and, like God, expected nothing in return except the joy of keeping our word?

You can be a one-sided Covenant keeper. Don't let the memories of times when people failed you, keep you from the blessings of Covenant. Don't stop there. Take a step of faith and become a one-sided Covenant maker! Set your eyes on Christ as you let your passion for Him compel you. Make promises to pray for people, and then do it. Press on when others would have given up. Believe the best and give the best. Sacrifice without the promise of glory. Be a **Keeper of Salt!**

> *Faithfulness is not a two-sided Covenant. Rather, it is a commitment to remain faithful even if the other party is not.*

If we have got the true love of God shed abroad in our hearts, we will show it in our lives. We will not have to go up and down the earth proclaiming it. We will show it in everything we say or do.

— Dwight L. Moody

CHAPTER 12

THROUGH COVENANT EYES

Watch out! There comes another one. Oh no, did you see that? It looks like the king is mad. He is trying to kill you David!

What do you do when someone you love and respect starts to throw spears at you? How do you react? Where do you hide? Do you throw spears back? Do you have a few hidden knives of your own ready to throw? Are you hurt? Are you angry? Does resentment and bitterness look for a home in your heart?

Who do you see in the person throwing spears? Do you see an enemy? Or perhaps you see a friend who has gone crazy? Maybe you see a fellow Christian. Maybe the person throwing spears is a family member!

I wonder what went on in David's head. I wonder, didn't he just once start to throw a spear back at Saul? He could have. He probably had several weapons at his disposal. After all, he was a skilled warrior. He could have easily killed Saul. But David didn't retaliate. Instead, David saw that Saul had been anointed as his king. David's Covenant with God necessitated David's respect for God's anointed. David looked at Saul through Covenant eyes.

A young married couple came to Fred and I for counsel a few years ago. The few years they had been married had not been easy. Tempers often flared, and with them accusations and innuendos. As we sat down to talk, the young woman began to rage. Glaring at her husband, she began to verbally throw spears at him. I watched as the young man cowered. I could see he was hurt and discouraged because he loved his wife very much. I wondered how he could just sit and listen to this. It wasn't long before he began to throw his own verbal spears.

> *Sometime we get caught up in the fight and lose sight of the Covenant.*

For what seemed like hours, the couple shouted, ranted and raved. If Fred and I could have only helped them see that they really loved each other. But we could hardly be heard above their shouts and painful finger pointing. It became obvious to me that the couple could only see hurts and feelings of betrayal. They weren't looking at each other through Covenant eyes. Sadly, their marriage didn't last long.

If you only see spears, you will gladly pick them up and throw them back where they came from. Sometimes we get caught up in the fight and lose sight of the Covenant. But those who see with the eyes of Covenant see *the person* who is throwing the spears. They remember their Covenant to them and to God.

GOD IS OUR VINDICATOR

In the beginning years of our ministry, Fred and I spent a lot of time working with youth. We began to organize local Bible quizzing. At first we wrote, organized and administered the quizzes. However, as we started doing regional quizzing we realized that the workload was too much for us alone. We needed someone else to actually go out and administer the quizzes.

A couple volunteered, although it soon became apparent that the couple didn't like me. They continually criticized me, until it became difficult to even carry on a conversation with them without some confrontation.

Our problems climaxed at a big youth rally. There were several issues that they started to throw at me like spears. They wouldn't let the issues drop, and soon it became a big scene in the church. People were looking at us, and began to gather around. I was shocked at how upset this couple was.

To deflate the angry and emotional scene, we scheduled a meeting with the couple for the next day. I can remember how nervous and distressed I was before the meeting. Before going into the meeting, I remember the Lord speaking to my heart saying, "Don't defend yourself. Be quiet and let everyone else talk."

After church the next day, I found myself facing my accusers in the dreaded meeting. Soon all of the issues were brought out into the open. As the couple listed one problem after another, I never said a word. Each time an issue was brought up, I noticed that someone else in the room would claim responsibility for what had been done. By the end of the meeting, each issue had been resolved. I hadn't needed to respond at all because God had provided a way out for me.

Often the very person who is destined to be our friend or our greatest support offends us. When the offense happens, if I throw spears, I may kill my future Covenant friend! If all I see is an opportunity to get even or justify myself, then I may never see the real motive. The opportunity to throw spears is an opportunity for God to work in my heart. Covenant eyes recognize the hand of God on the offender's life, and realize that sometimes people don't know what they are doing. God isn't as interested in the spears that are thrown at me, as He is interested in how I will *react* to them. Can I look beyond the offense? Can I look past the hurt and see God? Do I have Covenant eyes?

Sometimes I have found myself mulling over destructive, spear-like, thoughts toward those who have hurt me. I pick up a spear and twirl it around in my hands for a while. I'm sure if I let it fly I would hit my mark. But then I'm reminded of when God told me to keep my mouth shut. I remember that God is my vindicator. I am reminded that it's not my battle, but His.

It happens to all of us. Sometimes we let the spears fly, to hurt those who have hurt us. We stop looking at others with Covenant eyes, and start looking with our natural eyes. We are blinded by our bruised hearts. It isn't always easy to look with Covenant eyes. It is a choice. We have to choose to not look through the eyes of offense but look through the eyes of Covenant.

I could have thrown a lot of spears and pointed out the faults of that couple. I could have wounded them by responding through a spirit of offense. But my Covenant with God prevented me. I couldn't look at the situation through the eyes of offense. Instead, I looked through the eyes of Covenant and kept my mouth shut. I let God be my vindicator.

Covenant eyes can say with Stephen while he was being stoned, "Father, don't hold these accountable, because they don't know what they are doing." [1] Covenant eyes say with Jesus when He cried out from the cross, "Father, forgive them, for they don't know what they are doing." [2]

How do you respond when you are attacked? Do you see spears as an opportunity to wound those who have wounded you, or have you put on "heavenly contact lenses" and see wounded people who need their Covenant friend now more than ever?

God isn't as interested in the spears that were thrown at me, as He is interested in how I will react to them. Can I look past the hurt and see God?

Choose today to see people as God sees them. Choose to put on Covenant eyes. Let the offense and the hurt go. Allow God to be your vindicator. Allow Him to do His work in your life. Be a **Keeper of Salt**!

A family is a place where prin-
ciples are hammered and honed
on the anvil of everyday living.

— Charles R. Swindoll

CHAPTER 13

FAMILY

The young girl on the school bus was about fifteen years old. When I looked at her, I noticed that she was crying. I was a senior in high school and a few years older than she was, so I didn't really know her, but I walked up to her and asked her what was wrong.

She said, "My dad threw me out of the house this morning because I told him I thought I was pregnant. I have no place to go, and I don't know what to do."

"Don't worry", I replied. "Just come home with me. I'm sure everything will be all right."

That night after school, she did just that. I knew it would be okay for her to come home with me.

Later that night, my mom and dad said to me, "Debby, if you ever get into trouble, if you ever do things you shouldn't do, remember you can always come home."

The young girl only stayed for a few days, and when she found out she wasn't pregnant, she went back to her home. Her visit didn't last long, but I'll never forget what my mom and dad said. It's one thing to know something instinctively; it's another to be told conclusively. I never had to wonder or worry like my new young friend. My parents were Covenant people, and nothing I did or didn't do would ever change that.

I learned a lot about Covenant while growing up. I didn't know it was Covenant back then, but that's what it

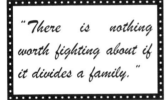

"There is nothing worth fighting about if it divides a family."

was. My mother has told me many times, "There is nothing worth fighting about if it divides a family." She means it, too. She's very careful to maintain relationships.

I know some families who are always fighting and don't speak to each other for years. I'm reminded of my mother's words. No family should be divided. Family is the home of Covenant. It's where Covenant should be born, taught and lived.

When we got our new house in Africa, our daughter Marie-Louise had her own bedroom. It was the first time she had ever slept alone, and she was a little afraid. One night shortly after we moved in, we had a powerful thunderstorm. On the first clap of the thunder Fred jumped out of bed and ran down the stairs to Marie-Louise's doorway. He arrived just as the thunder rang out in fury. It was so loud that it shook the house.

Marie-Louise cried out, "Daddy, where are you?"

Fred rushed in, gathered her up in his arms and said, "I was here before you called. I knew you might be afraid."

What a wonderful lesson he taught Marie-Louise. I hope she never forgets it. Fred was there before she called out, and God is always there even before we call Him. It's part of the Covenant!

I learned Covenants from my family. Probably my best friends growing up were my mom, dad, sister and brother. I didn't do a lot with my friends at school because my life was so full at home. We did a lot of things as a family. We went to parks, sang, shopped, cooked and went to church together. They were, and still are my Covenant friends. What could be better than going out for breakfast with my sister, trying out a new recipe with my mom, going to the beach with my brother, or traveling singing with my dad? Our Covenant had made wonderful family memories, and it promises more to come.

> *God is always there even before we call Him. It's part of the Covenant!*

I know some people who say that parents aren't meant to be friends to their children. But where better to learn Covenant friendship than at home? This reminds me of when a woman told me that I couldn't have friends in the church as a pastor's wife. Some people say that if you are friends with your children, they won't respect you. But that wasn't the way it was for me. I don't think there is anyone whom I respect more than my mom and dad.

FROM MASTER TO FRIEND

When our son Christopher was small, I was the master. However, as he grew it gradually became less of a dictatorship and more of a friendship. As I became his friend, he continued to respect me and treat me with the greatest of kindness. Today he's not only my son, but he is also one of my best friends. It was never my desire to forever be a master, but that someday he and I would have the same relationship that I have today with my mom and dad.

The progression from master to friend as a parenting principle can also be seen in the way God relates with us. When God first gave the Law to Moses, His relationship with man became one of rules and laws. But those who became mature in their relationship with Him (i.e. David, Jeremiah and Daniel), realized it wasn't about the rules and laws, but about Covenant-relationship. Even in **Deuteronomy**, God said He was looking for those who would love Him with their whole being.[1] **Galatians 3:24** says that the Law was our schoolteacher bringing us to Christ. The law existed for the purpose of bringing us into Covenant Friendship with Him. His goal wasn't the law; His goal was Covenant!

Growing up with Covenant gives a child a lot of security. It also teaches a child priceless lessons about the Covenant faithfulness of God. Things learned at home follow us the rest of our lives. Often we inadvertently transfer our experiences, good or bad, to God when we are grown. That's why it's so sad when children grow up in bad home situations. So many adults have a hard time trusting God in heaven because they have never learned to trust their parents at home.

I was teaching on Covenant in a bible school in Africa when one of the young pastors raised his hand to ask a question.

"What hope is there for me?" he asked. "I grew up in a home that practiced witchcraft, where my parents have made wicked Covenants. They have no respect for God."

I immediately reminded him of the story of David, a man who loved God with all of his heart. We have no record of whether or not his mother and father were devoted to the Lord, but we do know that they were among the generation of Israel that rejected God. For generations before David, the Israelites had forgotten the Lord and worshiped other gods. Yet because of God's mercy, David was able to rise above the sins of his parent's generation, and become a Covenant man after the heart of God.

We read in the book of Judges that the Children of Israel forgot to remind their children about their Covenant with God. They were instructed to tell them about the Covenant when they came into their houses and when they went out. They were to tell them over and over again, when they sat down to eat and when they went to bed. But they forgot, and generation after generation was sold into slavery.

Don't be like the Children of Israel. Regardless of your past, you can affect the next generation. You may not have had a childhood like mine, but you have the power to teach Covenant to those who follow after you. Of all the things we can teach our children, a Covenant with God is the only thing which is eternal. Make your home the place where your children learn about Covenant. Give them an eternal gift. Teach them to train the next generation, and the next. Family is a wonderful place to teach Covenant. It is where you learn to be a **Keeper of Salt**.

Regardless of your past, you can affect the next generation.

NOTES:

A friend is one who comes in when the whole world has gone out.

A friend will joyfully sing with you when you are on the mountaintop, and silently walk beside you through the valley.

— Anonymous

CHAPTER 14

COVENANTS OF AFFLICTION

For years I held a women's Bible study in my home. We enjoyed something very special. Whenever anyone had a need, we all gathered around and prayed. If one of us was in trouble, we all cried. If one rejoiced, we all rejoiced. I shared with them my fears of pastoral friendship, and they accepted me with no questions asked. It was a wonderful group! All week I would look forward to our meeting.

When I found out I had cancer, those women were there for me. Two of my Bible study friends, Cathy and Nancy, traveled over three hours to the hospital, and then tromped into my room wearing old hiking boots and matching bathrobes. I laughed so hard that I had to hold myself together to keep from splitting my stitches! They brought shopping bags full of gag gifts wrapped in used Christmas wrap. They were the talk of the hospital, and the highlight of my day. They didn't want me to be the only one wearing nightclothes. They were willing to dress like fools for my sake.

When I came home from the hospital, I was surprised to see my entire den changed from a den to a lovely downstairs bedroom.

> *Troubles do more than just develop our character, they prove our friends.*

The ladies in the church had gathered curtains, pictures, even a daybed, and had placed them in my newly "remodeled" den. These women sacrificed for me. My friend Peg came twice from Ohio to be with me, and the other women all made arrangements to take turns caring for me when she wasn't there. Cathy came every day just to check on me and pray for me. Every one of these women proved their friendship in those days of trouble. I cannot talk about Covenant friends without mentioning these women. I wish I could tell you stories about them all, but that would be a whole book by itself!

This is how Covenant friends act. They do whatever it takes to see their Covenant friend blessed. They don't care how much it costs or how much time it takes. Most importantly though, Covenant friends take care of each other in times of trouble. Troubles do more than just develop our character; they prove our friends.

Troubles have a way of finding new friends for us. People feel *connected* when they meet someone who has been through the same troubles as they. Alcoholics join AA. The parents of children who have died from Sudden Infant Death Syndrome join a SIDS support group. Soldiers who have been though a war together have an unmistakable camaraderie between them. There is a mysterious connection between people who has been through similar hardships. For friends, this connection is often a Covenant of affliction.

My friend Judy and I have faced many battles together. We have a unique friendship because it has grown stronger under stressful situations. We've walked for miles on dusty roads in Africa, in the scorching heat. We've prayed for hundreds of hurting women. We've even cleaned rotting teeth on dental missions. However, perhaps we felt the most connected when we realized that we had both gone through similar battles with cancer. There have been days when we have both felt like giving up, but through it all, our friendship remains strong. Our afflictions have brought us together. It's no surprise to me that we have developed a Covenant friendship.

David and Jonathan also had a Covenant of affliction. Their friendship is legendary, but it was birthed out of the skirmish with Goliath, and maintained through unrelenting situations of trauma and apprehension. Their Covenant was proven in trouble. King Saul, Jonathan's father, had broken his Covenants with God and with David. As a result, an evil spirit tormented him. He was angry that Jonathan had made a Covenant with David; so angry that he tried to kill Jonathan. [1] What an awkward situation David and Jonathan found themselves in. What better example of a Covenant of affliction.

Jonathan could have told David, "I'm sorry, but you know how it is. My dad is the king and he doesn't want me to be your friend anymore. Besides, if I stay your friend, I may lose my place on the throne. Find someone else to be your friend!"

But that's not how the story reads. Jonathan said to David, "...we have sworn Covenant friendship to each other and the Lord is our witness. Someday, you will be king and I will be second to you." [2]

There have been people, whom I thought were Covenant friends, who have disappeared at the first sight of trouble. But this was not the case with Jonathan and David. Jonathan honored the Covenant, though it cost him everything, even the throne. Troubles had proven the depth of his friendship. The price he paid was great.

Every Covenant suffers some kind of trouble. When Jesus was on trial and faced crucifixion, the Covenant His followers had with Him was tried. Would they stay with their Lord or would they cower away in fear? Peter came close by denying Jesus three times, but came through in the end. Peter's Covenant was being tried in the fires of affliction. Jesus even prayed for Peter, that his "faith would not fail".[3] After Jesus rose from the dead, He called for Peter to reestablish their Covenant. Nothing would ever tempt Peter to deny this relationship again. He suffered greatly and even went to prison because of his Covenant, but he never denied Jesus again. Peter had become a **Keeper of Salt**.

A true Covenant friend will stay with you, no matter the impact of trial. Proverbs tells us that a friend loves at all times, and that there is a friend who sticks closer than a brother.[4] Cathy is this type of friend. Fred and I went through a difficult season in our lives in which experienced an overload of criticism. Worse than that when "the going got tough" most of our "friends" left – except for Cathy. She stood by me when others did not. The fires of trouble have proven her friendship and reaffirmed our Covenant.

Make no mistake; *trouble itself* does not separate Covenant friends. All relationships go through times of trouble. Rather, it's bad attitudes and offenses that break Covenant friendships. It's when we allow emotion and the craze-of-the-moment to dictate our response that our friendships are in danger. In the time of trouble, the separation of two covenant friends is a willful choice, not an inevitable result. Remember, God is greater than any storm your Covenant may go through.

> *In the time of trouble, the separation of two covenant friends is a willful choice, not an inevitable result.*

THICKER THAN MILK

People have asked me if "sin" is a good enough reason to break a Covenant friendship. There is no doubt that sin strains friendships. I know people who have "written off" old, longtime friends, because "they have backslidden" or because "they are living in idolatry". No doubt these are sins. Nonetheless, do they provide sufficient reason to break Covenant?

You might have heard the expression, "Blood is thicker than water." This is understood to mean that the relationship one has with their sister or brother, is stronger than any relationship they have with someone else. There was a similar saying in the ancient oriental culture, "Blood is thicker than milk."[5] To them this meant that,

Blood Covenant is stronger than any other relationship, even the relationship of a brother or sister who drank milk from the same breast. The ancient Orientals understood that no one, not even a relative, can break Covenant. No matter the difficulty, no matter the sin, nothing can separate those in Covenant. Of course, if your Covenant friend is living in a sinful lifestyle or is committing self-destructive acts, you may (and probably should) disagree with them. Tell them that you disapprove of their actions. But *someone* has to love them enough to help them change, and if you are in Covenant with that person, you are that one! You might be surprised at how often someone is waiting for words of love and acceptance. Christ-like people will refuse to tear apart from their friends, they will *restore* them. Restoration is part of the Covenant, and it's a major theme of the New Testament.[6] Remember, it's God's *kindness* that leads us to repentance.[7]

Not only should we maintain our Covenant friendships through the storms of life, but God wants to give us new Covenant friends in the midst of those problems. As you read this, you may find yourself in the middle of a storm. Don't give up! Unexpected blessings could be just around the corner. Look for opportunities to love someone. You never know when your act of love could turn into a wonderful new Covenant friendship. Don't allow affliction to steal your Covenants; rather allow it to make them stronger. Only during adversity do we see who truly is, a **Keeper of Salt**!

NOTES:

Covenant love is the driving force of our faith.

— Cheryl Harrison

CHAPTER 15

THE PLACE OF COVENANT

In the days even before Abraham, people practiced what was called the *Threshold Covenant.*[1] In this Covenant, once a guest had stepped over the threshold or entry place of a house, he came into Covenant with the owner of the house.[2] Nothing could break this Covenant. The guest could not hurt the owner of the house in any way, and the owner was obligated to protect the guest, even at the cost of his own life.

People of the *Ga tribe* in Ghana West Africa, practice a unique type of the Threshold Covenant. Whenever they are in need of a new king, the leaders of the tribe meet in secret and decide who the next king shall be. Then they sacrifice a cow in the doorway, letting the blood run across the threshold. The leaders then carry the chosen man upon their shoulders over the threshold. Once the man crosses the threshold, he becomes their king, and the tribe comes into an unbreakable Covenant with him.[3]

In some ancient cultures, when a king would travel through his land, he would seek for those who were loyal to him. If the subjects of his kingdom knew he was coming, they would offer a sacrifice in their doorways and place the blood on the doorposts. Even from a distance, the king would be able to see the blood, and he would know that these people were loyal to him. If the king came to a certain house and stepped over the bloody threshold, it meant he wanted to come into blood Covenant with the man of the house. Because of the Covenant, the man of the house would gladly give his life for the king.[4]

In the book of Exodus we see a similar example of Threshold Covenants. Moses commanded the Israelites to place blood on their doorposts as a sign of their Covenant with God. This procedure was not a new concept to the Israelites. It meant the King was coming! According to biblical historians, the Death Angel passed over the Israelite's houses, and the King, God Himself, entered. God passed over the bloody threshold, and reestablished a Covenant with a people who had forgotten Him.[5]

> *Jesus stands at the door of our hearts and knocks. Will you let him over your threshold? Will you be His Covenant friend?*

The Bible says that Jesus stands at the door of our hearts and knocks.[6] Will you let him over your threshold? Will you be His Covenant friend? Will you be willing to give your life for him?

THE POWER COVENANT

Lot found himself in the wicked cities of Sodom and Gomorrah. The Bible tells us that the angels of the Lord came to these cities, and Lot found them and brought them home with him. Later that evening, wicked men came and wanted to molest Lot's visitors. Lot refused their offer, and instead, he offered his virgin daughters.[7]

Why would someone offer their daughters as a substitute for two strangers? The answer lies in the power of Covenant. The key phrase we often miss is found in **Genesis 19:8**. "For they have come under the protection of my roof." When these angels came over Lot's threshold, Lot came into Covenant with them. He wasn't being a cruel father, sending his daughters off to be molested; Lot was performing His Covenant duty. In effect, he was saying, "These men have come through my doorway. They have stepped over the blood of the Covenant. I must protect them, even at the expense of my most precious possession. I have two daughters who are pure. And so, I offer them to you. Take them, but do not harm my guests because I have given them my Covenant of protection."[8]

I have included this story to illustrate that our culture doesn't understand the depths of Covenant. We would never consider sacrificing a child. In Lot's culture, the obligations of Covenant were so highly valued that they even superceded the relationship between a man and his children. Remember it is said in **II Peter 2:7** that Lot was righteous. It's hard for us to comprehend this but again this shows our confusion regarding the power of Covenant. I don't know how a man could even consider to sacrifice his child, nor am I suggesting that you *should* sacrifice your children, however remember Abraham too was ready to sacrifice his only son Isaac, for the sake of his Covenant.

Sound familiar? It should. God did the same for us. He found us wandering in our sin, and He offered us protection in His house. The Blood of Jesus was sacrificed and we, by faith, stepped over a bloody cross, into eternal life with Him. When the devil came looking for us, to molest and destroy us, God said, "Look, my guests have entered my house. They have stepped over the Blood of the Covenant. I am obligated by the Covenant to give my protection. I must protect them, even if it costs me my most precious possession. I have a Son. He is pure and there is no sin in Him. You may take Him, but you can not touch those who have come into Covenant with me."

The power of Covenant. It's strong enough to make God give up His Son. God's Covenant love pursues us, even in our sin. His love is entirely committed to us. It is stronger than any offense, any storm, any sickness, any problem we may ever face. Covenant is the reason for Communion. Those who keep Covenant enjoy abundant blessings and vibrant lives. Those who break it suffer depravity in their relationships with God and man. Covenant is powerful, with power to bless or curse your life.

In these last days, it is time for the Church worldwide to end her years of disjointed "unity". The Body of Christ is a bride who has *forgotten* her vows. It is time for isolated, offended and hurting people to realize that their commitment to Christ is also their Covenant to their brothers and sisters. Covenant is calling the church back to her groom. It is calling people to mend their differences, and reconcile with their offenders. It is then that the Church will be a "glorious body, without spot or wrinkle". Because Covenant is powerful, it will change the church.

The blessings of Covenant await those who will be true to it. In a world of broken promises, *Covenant* must distinguish the people of God from all others. It is the missing key to the "fruitful and victorious" Christian life we so often hear about on Sunday morning. Covenant will breathe peace into our homes and lives, reunite our families and friends, and lead us to the "greater things" Jesus promised. Covenant is our calling. It is our purpose in life. It is powerful, and it will change your life.

Now it's time for you to be a **Keeper of Salt**.

> *The blessings of Covenant await those who will be true to it. In a world of broken promises, Covenant must distinguish the people of God from all others.*

EPILOGUE

I had planned a special weekend with a few of my friends. I was in the States while my husband Fred was in Africa, so I decided it would be a great time for a women's get-together. When I first started planning the weekend, I thought that four or five women would come. My plan was to share what God had been speaking to me about Covenant. However, as the date got closer and word got out, I realized that a lot more people were coming. I soon realized that I was going to have somewhere between thirty-five and fifty friends arriving for my weekend sleepover.

As the sleepover date drew closer, it became apparent that the little guest apartment, where Fred and I stay when we are in America, was too small for so many people. Since the apartment is a part of my father's church, I began to look for other places in the church for all these women to sleep. We also needed another shower. The church has a lot of rooms, and my father thought that there might be an old shower in the basement. We started snooping around and sure enough, there was indeed a shower in the basement. The room it was in however was a mess. There were old toilets and pipes going everywhere. Since No one had used the room for years, it was moldy and creepy.

My father and my sister's husband, Guy, went to work cleaning up the shower room. They boarded up windows, tacked up insulation and hauled out garbage until you could finally see the floor. Then I went to work painting. With my friend Cathy's help we decorated the shower room and the rest of the basement rooms in preparation for the weekend sleepover. We planned to have meals in the basement and then have everyone sleep in the first floor dining room. The guest apartment is on the second floor, and since it is a very old building with long flights of stairs, I was climbing a lot.

I have had trouble with my knees for years. By the end of the first cleaning and painting week, my knees were sore. By the end of the second week they were very sore, and I had the weekend yet to look forward to! I was climbing up and down those stairs many, many times a day. I knew that I would be sore and tired out. I knew there was a price I was paying, but I wanted to do it. I loved these women, so I wanted the place to look nice for them when they came. Because it was going to be a special weekend, I was willing to pay the price of sore knees for my friends. What I didn't know was that by the end of the sleepover, after everyone had left and gone home, my knees would be trembling so bad that I would hardly be able to get up the stairs to the guest apartment.

Greater love hath no man than this, that a man lay down his life for his friends. **John 15:13**

On Saturday night of the sleep over, we celebrated communion together. As I broke the bread and began to distribute it to my friends, I began to think about Jesus when He broke the bread for His disciples. When Jesus broke the bread, He told His disciples that it was His body broken for them. Only hours later, Jesus hung on the cross. His body had indeed been broken for His friends. As I broke the bread that night I remembered that Jesus wanted me to do the same. Was I willing to be broken for my friends? I felt my tired and sore knees and in my heart said, "Yes". As I broke the bread I said, "This is my body broken for you." Jesus' words had become more than echoed words and more real than solemn memories. I had applied Communion to my life. I wanted to be like Jesus. I wanted my Covenant friends to know that I was willing to lay down my life, move past my feelings, change my agenda, and adjust my desires for them. Later the next day, nursing my sore knees, Jesus whispered to me and said, "See, you were willing to be broken for your friends."

Keeping salt is what you do every day. It's a phone call to the relative you haven't spoken to in years. It's the plate of food you send to a widow next door. It's the note of appreciation you send to your pastor, even when you didn't like last week's message. Keeping salt is what I did on that weekend with my friends. It's a way of life.

Keep therefore the words of this Covenant, and do them, that ye may prosper in all that ye do. **Deuteronomy 29:9**

ENDNOTES

Preface

1. Names changed
2. "The Salt Covenant" by Dr. H. Clay Trumbull Impact Christian Books; pages 15-18
3. "The Salt Covenant" pages 104, 102

Chapter 1

1. Quote from Richard Wright author of "A More Excellent Way"
2. Jacob Milgrom, "The JPS Torah Commentary": Numbers (Philadelphia: Jewish Publication Society of America, 1990), p. 154. www.jhom.com
3. "The Salt Covenant" pages 21-30
4. "The Salt Covenant" page 129
5. Pastor Beugre Ebi Salomon of Abidjan, Ivory Coast; as quoted on June 11, 2003
6. Matthew 5:13   "The Salt Covenant" page 67
7. AN EXPOSITION OF THE OLD and NEW TESTAMENT; IN NINE VOLUMES BY JOHN GILL, D.D. PRINTED FOR MATHEWS AND LEIGH, 18 STRAND, LONDON by W. Clowes, Northumberland-Court 1809 Edited and revised and updated by Larry Pierce, 1994- 1995. "Gill's Notes" Titus 1:2
8. Geneses 1:1-3
9. Genesis 8:22
10. "The Salt Covenant", page 39, 49, 51, 57, 58
11. Latin word from page 44 of "The Salt Covenant" by H. Clay Trumbull
12. Genesis 15:9; 17:23-27

13. "The Blood Covenant", "The Salt Covenant", and "The Threshold Covenant "by Trumbull, Impact Christian Books; "The Blood Covenant" by E.W. Kenyon

14. "The Blood Covenant"; Understanding the Blood of the Covenant by Jack Hayford

15. "The Blood Covenant" page 218; James 2:23

16. "The Blood Covenant" page 215-223, 240

17. Genesis 15:5 17:3-8, 22:17

18. "The Blood Covenant" by Trumbull page 264-265

19. "The Blood Covenant" by Trumbull page 6

20. This information comes from Pastor Nazaire A. Hounkpadode, Pastor/President of EEDSC Church, Cotonou, Benin, West Africa.

21. "The Covenants" by Kevin Conner and Ken Malmin, City Bible Publishing   page 4-7

22. Genesis 17:1; Genesis 17:9-14

23. Genesis 17:11

24. Matthew 4:7,10, Deuteronomy 8:3, 6:16,13

25. Judges 2:10, 20; 3:7, 12; 4:1; 6:1; 8:33-34; 10:6; 13:1

26. New International Version, KJV John 14:12

Chapter 2

1. Macgregor's Rob Roy on the Jordan page 259, "The Salt Covenant" page 29, Microsoft ® En carta ® Reference Library 2002. © 1993-2001 Microsoft Corporation. All rights reserved.

2. "The Salt Covenant" page 41

3. "The Salt Covenant" page 33

4. "The Blood Covenant" by Trumbull page 271-286

5. "The Blood Covenant" by Trumbull page 278
6. "The Blood Covenant" by Trumbull page 273
7. "The Salt Covenant" page 111
8. Romans 5:8-12; "The Blood Covenant" by Trumbull ; pages 286-293
9. "The Covenants" page 7
10. Gill's Notes; Family New Testament Notes; Barn's New Testament notes
11. "The Salt Covenant", painting of Judas and spilling salt page 104
12. "Strong's Exhaustive Concordance"
13. "Jamieson, Fausset, Brown Commentary"
14. "Blessing or Curse You Can Choose" Chosen a division of Baker Book House page 151
15. "Blessing or Curse You Can Choose" pages 121-134, 151, "Justification" Microsoft Encarta Encyclopedia 2001 copyright 1993-2000 Micro   soft Corporation.
    All rights reserved
16. "The Blood Covenant" page 285
17. "The Salt Covenant" page 22
18. Ephesians 5:2; Hebrews 9:26; 10:12

Chapter 3
1. From Richard Wright pastor and author of, "A More Excellent Way"

Chapter 4
1. Hebrews 12:15
2. Psalms 147:3; Isaiah 61:1; Proverbs 25:22; Jeremiah 17:10
3. Hebrews 4:15
4. John chapters 18,19

Chapter 5
1. Jonah 4:2
2. Luke 9:54-56
3. "Gill's Notes" Titus 3:2
4. Exodus 20:12
5. Matthew 19:26; Mark 10:27; Luke 1:37, 18:27
6. Acts 9:13-14, 20,21,26
7. Ephesians 5:21
8. 1 Samuel 24:5
9. Exodus 22:28; 1 Samuel 24:6, 26:9-11
   Romans 13:1; Titus 3:1; 1 Peter 2:13, 14, 17;
   Jude 8, Proverbs 21:1; Jude 10,
   Romans 13:1,5
10. Romans 8:28

Chapter 6
1. Matthew 18:19,20
2. II Samuel 11
3. "Jamieson Fausset Brown Commentary",
   Hebrew The Hebrew favors "garment," being
   accusative of the thing covered.
   "Amplified Bible"
4. 11 Samuel 12:7-12
5. 1 Samuel 28:7-22
6. Psalms 51

Chapter 7
1. Corinthians 9:6,7; Galatians 6:7, Luke 6:38;
   Matthew 8:10; Acts 20:38 Romans 12:8
2. Luke 6:38
3. John 12:23-28
4. Luke 3: 11
5. Matthew 25:40

6. Lamentations 3:23
7. Matthew 19:26; Mark 10:27
8. Matthew 5:17
9. Matthew 22:37; Mark 12:30; Mark 12:33; Luke 10:27
10. Matthew 7:12; Matthew 22:36-40

Chapter 8

1. "Gill's Notes" Numbers 6:2
2. Judges 13:3-5
3. Numbers 6:1-8
4. 11 Corinthians 6:16,17
5. Numbers 6:19-21
6. Judges 14:1-3; Joshua 23:12-13
7. Genesis 50:20
8. Judges 14:6,8
9. Judges 15:15; Leviticus 11:20-28
10. 1 Samuel 1:10,11; 24-28
11. II Corinthians 5:17

Chapter 9

1. Deuteronomy 28:20, 28, 34, 65
2. 1 Chronicles 10:13
3. 1 Samuel 24:11
4. 1 Corinthians 13:4-8
5. 1 Samuel chapters 24 and 26
6. 11 Samuel 15
7. 11 Samuel 18:5,33-19:1-8
8. 11 Samuel 15:25
9. John 17:21

Chapter 10
1. "Gill's Notes" Acts 15:36-41
2. "The Salt Covenant" page   104
3. II Timothy 2:23; Titus 3:9
4. "Gill's Notes" Malachi 3:16

Chapter 12
1. Acts 7:60
2. Luke 23:34

Chapter 13
1. Deuteronomy 6:5; 10:12; 11:13; 13:3 30:6

Chapter 14
1. 1 Samuel 20:33; 22:8
2. 1 Samuel 20:42; 23:17-18
3. Luke 22:32
4. Proverbs 17:17; 18:24; 27:6
5. "The Blood Covenant" by Trumbull page 11
6. Galatians 6:2
7. Romans 2:4 NIV translation

Chapter 15
1. "The Threshold Covenant" by Dr. H. Clay
   Trumbull page 5, 107, 108;
   This is the place of Covenant See Geneses
   19:6-11; Exodus 12:22,23;21:6; 32:26; 33:9;
   40:6; Leviticus 1:3,5; 3:2; 4:4,7; 8:1-36;
   12:6;14:11,23; 15:14,29,16:7; 17:2-9;19:21;
   Numbers 6:10-18; John 10:7,9; Revelation 4:1;
   Judges 19:20-23; 11 Samuel 9:6-13
2. "The Threshold Covenant" page 5
3. Pastor Manford Amasah, Accra, Ghana, Africa
   as told on August 2003

4. "The Threshold Covenant" pages 186-189
5. Exodus 12:22-23; 21:6
6. Revelation 3:20
   Genesis 19:6
   "The Threshold Covenant" page 192,
   "Gill's Notes" on verses 4-14,
   Craig Hill Family Foundations, "The Blood
   Covenant", Audio Covenant Series I II
   Family Foundations Colorado

NOTE: Even today there are modern day examples of the Threshold Covenant. In the country of Senegal in West Africa, the President has erected a statue with a door at the base that whenever anyone enters through this statue's doorway, they have entered into Covenant with him. There is no blood involved in this statue, but it is symbolic of the Threshold Covenant where the blood is sacrificed in the doorway and Covenant is made. This information comes from Pastor Michel Silva Andrade, Dakar, Senegal, Africa.

In Abomey, Benin, Africa, when a stranger enters a house, the woman of the house will bow down greeting the stranger with a basin of water, which she pours out on the ground of the doorway. When the person enters, he walks through the water and enters into Covenant with the people of the house. From Pastor Martial Ahannon

11300465R00103

Made in the USA
San Bernardino, CA
13 May 2014